THE PERILS OF A PASTOR'S WIFE

IF GOD BE FOR ME, WHO CAN BE AGAINST ME?

By
Nan Jones

Sweet blessings to you,
Nan Jones
Exodus 33:14

Straight Street Books
Lighthouse Publishing of the Carolinas

THE PERILS OF A PASTOR'S WIFE BY NAN JONES
Published by Straight Street Books
An imprint of Lighthouse Publishing of the Carolinas
2333 Barton Oaks Dr., Raleigh, NC 27614

ISBN: 978-1-941103-77-7
Copyright © 2015 by Nan Jones
Cover design by Goran Tomic
Interior design by AtriTeX Technologies P Ltd

Available in print from your local bookstore, online, or from the publisher at:
www.lighthousepublishingofthecarolinas.com

For more information on this book and the author visit: NanJones.com

Brought to you by the creative team at LighthousePublishingoftheCarolinas.com: Denise Loock, Cindy Sproles, Eddie Jones, and Shonda Savage.

Library of Congress Cataloging-in-Publication Data
Jones, Nan.
The Perils of a Pastor's Wife / Nan Jones 1st ed.

Printed in the United States of America

Praise for *The Perils of a Pastor's Wife*

I so appreciate Nan Jones' heart for pastors' wives. Every chapter of *The Perils of a Pastor's Wife* expresses that tender heart so sweetly. And each chapter takes us right to God's Word—exactly what we need for finding wisdom, comfort, and victory in our calling as ministers' wives.

Rhonda Rhea

TV host, and author of *Join the Insanity: Crazy-Fun Life in the Pastors' Wives Club*

Through *The Perils of a Pastor's Wife*, my well-worn heart was lightened and encouraged. In its pages, a fellow life traveler finds tons of hope for the inevitable perils of life. We are allowed to laugh, nod, and cry out with Nan Jones as she seeks to know God in the midst of her circumstances. God tendered the trampled places of my heart as I joined Nan in her story. While relating to women in ministry, *The Perils of a Pastor's Wife* will benefit any Christian wife that has endured spiritual loneliness, harsh betrayal, secret suffering, or divine silence. It's simply a great return to God's priorities!

Robin Bryce

Minister's wife, speaker, and author of Confessions of a Preacher's Wife blog

The Perils of a Pastor's Wife speaks life into weary souls who, day in and out, stand beside their pastor-husband and engage in the battle with him. From years of real-life experience, Nan Jones declares the truth she had to hang on to in order to survive in the face of pastoral abuse, misunderstanding, and betrayal. Her words will bring needed rest for many souls. If you're married to a pastor, read this book. If you're considering marrying a pastor, oh, please, read this book. And for the rest of you, please buy a copy for your pastor's wife. I promise it will be an answer to prayer.

Athena Dean Holtz
Author, speaker, radio personality,
publisher, and pastor's wife

In *The Perils of a Pastor's Wife*, Nan Jones comes clean about her experience in the ministry. Was she married to the minister or married to the ministry? It's part exposé, part autobiography. Nan embraces the reader like an encouraging girlfriend in ministry, highlighting why we do what we do while not downplaying the difficult parts. She gets it—this life of ministry. Being married to a minister isn't easy, but it doesn't have to be as hard as we make it either. *The Perils of a Pastor's Wife* reveals the life lesson Nan has learned over and over again—that people will let us down, but God is faithful, and there's freedom in living life for an audience of One. If you've ever felt like no one understood what your life is like in ministry, this book is for you.

Kathy Carlton Willis
Pastor's wife, speaker,
and multi-published author, including *Grin with Grace*

Every person in full-time ministry needs this book! Nan Jones has lived the perils, experiencing the blessings and the hardships involved in pastoral ministry. Her ability to stay nestled next to the Lord's heart in spite of pain will refresh and encourage you immeasurably.

Nancy LaPointe
Author of *Living in God's Rest ... At Peace in a Chaotic World*

What a great book of encouragement for pastors' wives! This book can encourage every pastor's wife, no matter what her circumstances are. Many times a wife may feel she has no one to talk to who understands her challenges and who won't turn against her and create more problems for her. Nan Jones shares from her experiences how she made the decision to grow through it all rather than to be paralyzed with fear, rejection, disappointment, loss, or other attacks of the enemy. She shares insights into the husband/wife relationship in ministry and how God can enable couples to become stronger when they allow Him to take their roots deeper and choose to respond with His grace. You'll be inspired to overcome when you read this book.

Pastor Sharon Daugherty
Founding pastor, Victory Christian Center, Tulsa, OK, author, speaker, and television host

The Perils of a Pastor's Wife is an amazing masterpiece of the life of ministry couples. Nan Jones mercifully shares the "dark side" and "the dark night of the soul" that many ministry wives experience but are afraid to share. She gives our silent sisters a voice so the world will know that we too have had our share of bloodshed. Any pastor's wife can share in the joy and pain of Nan's incredible journey and walk away with a new understanding of God's faithfulness.

Domeniek Harris
Pastor's wife and founder of By His Side Ministries
www.byhissideministries.org

Dedication

To my sisters who stand faithfully by their husbands
through the lonely fires of ministry,
undergirding them with their love.

TABLE OF CONTENTS

Acknowledgments

In Andrae´ Crouch's seventies' song classic, "My Tribute," he asks how we can offer adequate thanks when we see the hand of God moving mightily in our lives. It's difficult, isn't it? As I consider saying thanks to those who've supported me on my journey, the lyrics of "My Tribute" ramble through my mind … how can I say thanks?

The Lord has revealed to me many hidden treasures in the secret place beneath His wing. For that, I'm eternally grateful. He opened my eyes to see Him in the midst of my struggles—to *know* His Presence. He gave me a remarkable platform and an opportunity to minister to His ladies who serve on the front lines with their husbands, bringing His grace and love to a hurting world. For this gift, Lord, how can I say thanks?

Friends and family have stood with me, held my hands up when I was too tired to hold them up on my own. They prayed me through the stress of reliving painful experiences. They prayed that I would hear God's voice and write His message. Thank you to my husband, David, for teaching me to trust the Lord through all circumstances. Thank you to my children—Dave, Matthew, and Nancy—for believing in me and for those special hugs at just the right time. My sister-in-love, Carole, and her husband, Tom Gamble, thank you for faithfully cheering for me across the mountaintops. And to my mom, Mary Lee Trammell—your prayers have given me courage to fly. For your love, how can I say thanks?

Thank you, Judith Robl, one of my spiritual moms—you held my hand, protected my heart, and taught me the ways of forgiveness. Thank you, Lee McMillan, my landlord and friend. Through your generosity and kind heart, the Lord has made a way where there seemed to be no way. To my special friends—Jamie Britt, Tee-Tee Barnes, Norma Gail Thurston Holtman, and Marcie Bridges—wow! You ladies exemplify friendship. How many times have you been Jesus with skin on for me? Tee, you have stood with me in the good times and the bad, through the laughter and the tears. Jamie, you're the greatest little PR agent ever created. I cherish you. Norma, as another Lighthouse author, you have helped to guide me through this often complicated journey. Thank you for your friendship and your prayers. And Marcie, not only do I treasure your friendship, but also you have generously served as a knowledgeable extra set of eyes before I hit the "send" button. For your faithfulness, how can I say thanks?

Denise Loock, what a blessing you are to me. Thank you for taking my hand and walking with me through this maze of editing and for answering my endless questions with such grace. And thank you for holding my heart in friendship. Lighthouse Publishing of the Carolinas, you're a joy to work with. Thank you for your heart to honor God in all publishing matters. Eddie Jones, I appreciate your leadership as my publisher. Thank you also for the ministry you share with Cindy Sproles through Christian

Devotions. I count you both as gifts from heaven—tools to shape me into the writer God has called me to be. For your hearts to help others, how can I say thanks?

To Judy Hodge, my junkin' buddy and prayer warrior: you have prayed me through countless ministry nightmares and led me back to the light of His love. You're precious to me. For your laughter and love, how can I say thanks?

To each of you, I offer my sincere gratitude. I pray God's hand of favor on you and those you love. Continue to carry His love and laughter to a hurting world. Sweet blessings to you!

Author's Note:

Some names have been changed to protect
the identities of the people and churches mentioned
in the book.

Moreover whom He predestined, these He also called;
whom He called, these He also justified;
and whom He justified, these He also glorified.
What then shall we say to these things:

If God is for us,
who can be against us?

He who did not spare His own Son, but delivered Him up for us all,
how shall He not with Him also freely give us all things?

Who shall bring a charge against God's elect?
It is God who justifies.
It is Christ who died, and furthermore is also risen,
who is even at the right hand of God,
who also makes intercession for us.

Who shall separate us from the love of Christ?
Shall tribulation, or distress, or persecution, or famine,
or nakedness or peril or sword?

As it is written: "For Your sake we are killed all day long:
We are accounted as sheep for the slaughter."

Yet in all these things we are more than conquerors
through Him who loved us.
~ Romans 8:31-37

My Sister, I Know

My beloved sister, you do not walk alone. I know. I'm a pastor's wife too and well acquainted with the highs and lows of ministry. I've shared my husband with an endless stream of needy people. I've been consumed by loneliness in the midst of a crowd. I've kept my shield up, not knowing who can be fully trusted. I've experienced the heartbreak of pouring love and immeasurable grace into the lives of others, only to be spit upon with the poison of rejection by those who walk in self-righteousness.

My sister, I know.

I pray that *The Perils of a Pastor's Wife* will resonate within your spirit and give you strength for the journey. Through the pages of this book, you can find your validation and hope in God and in Him alone. When this truth becomes concrete in your *knower*, you'll no longer be tossed about by the whims of people. You may lose your balance momentarily when the fiery darts fly, but you'll regain your balance because you're a daughter of the King, called by His grace to minister alongside your husband.

May peace and security find you and bind up your wounds.

Father God, I lift my precious sister before Your mighty throne of grace. You're an awesome God, full of mercy and love. My sister needs to feel Your hand upon her. She needs to know Your grace is sufficient and Your promises are true. Lord, minister to her through the words of my heart—may my words be Your words. May Your daughter find wholeness and purpose once again. Thank You, Lord. We love You. You are our everything. Amen.

CHAPTER ONE

AFTER THE FIRE, A GENTLE WHISPER

Only God knew where my husband was. I had run from the business meeting before its completion. Tempers flared. Tongues were unleashed, and nearly three years of fruitful ministry were all but destroyed. My heart beat madly within my chest, fighting desperately not to break from the pain of rejection. Angry tears stung my cheeks as I bolted from the sanctuary. I didn't know if I could continue in this thing called ministry. God was asking too much of me.

My husband, David, and I had been ministering in the small rural church for three years. Under his leadership and the Holy Spirit's guidance, the church had experienced exponential growth. God's mercy and grace flowed into the lives of His people. Church had become a place of joy, restoration, and refuge.

Then evil reared its ugly head.

Church leaders who had controlled the congregation for decades felt threatened. The religious spirit that reigned in their hearts rose up and rebelled against the man of God. They conducted themselves much like the Pharisees of old, standing firm on law and tradition with little regard for the leading of the Holy Spirit. A fierce battle ensued. Hearts were torn. Young faith shattered. And, without a doubt, God removed His hand of blessing.

I hid in the parsonage until the meeting ended. When the last car pulled out of the parking lot, I sprinted toward the church, hoping no one saw me. I felt violated. Afraid. Condemned. David sat in his office seeking refuge in the Scriptures, so I tiptoed to the sanctuary. The church pew felt hard and cold against my body. Its chill reflected the tension pressing hard and cold against my spirit. Opening my Bible, I turned to 1 Kings 19:10-12:

> [Elijah] replied, "I have been very zealous for the LORD God Almighty. The Israelites have rejected your covenant, broken down your altars, and put your prophets to death with the sword. I am the only one left, and now they are trying to kill me too." The LORD said, "Go out and stand on the mountain in the presence of the LORD, for the LORD is about to pass by." Then a great and powerful wind tore the mountains apart and shattered the rocks before the LORD, but the LORD was not in the wind. After the wind there was an earthquake, but the LORD was not in the earthquake. After the earthquake came a fire, but the LORD was not in the fire. And after the fire came a gentle whisper.

"Oh my God, help me!" I pleaded as I fell to my knees. The cold wood of the altar sent shivers down my spine. Like Elijah, I spoke plainly to the Lord, "We've worked diligently for Your kingdom. These people are rebellious and stiff-necked. They have no respect for Your authority and no respect for Your servants. And now they seek to destroy us. Why, Lord? I don't understand."

Like Elijah, I'd had enough.

The Lord told Elijah to go out and stand on the mountain before Him. And then the Lord displayed His mighty power through a windstorm, an earthquake, and a fire. But God wasn't in any of those elements. God displayed His awesome power to His weary servant and then tenderly ministered to him with a still, small voice. While reflecting on this passage about Elijah, I discovered marginal notes in my study Bible that describe God's spoken word in these verses as "a delicate whispering voice."[1] God revealed Himself to His broken servant in a delicate whispering voice.

Oh, beloved sister, let this timeless truth sink in: God revealed Himself to His broken servant in a delicate whispering voice.

I love God's tenderness.

As I knelt at the altar, I remembered God's power in my life, the times He defended our family with His army of angels, the times money showed up in the mailbox or groceries appeared on the back stoop. I remembered the consuming fire of His Presence when the worshipers could not stand because of His glory.

At that moment, my Redeemer whispered to me gently:

Child, I love you. You suffer for my sake and you bring Me honor. I am your refuge in the storm, your strong tower. Run to Me and be safe. I am the Sovereign Lord, the Almighty God, and I have not forsaken you. I will make a way where there seems to be no way. I will shield and defend you by My Spirit and by the testimony of My Word. Do not be afraid. You are Mine.

I bowed before my Lord that night. His tenderness engulfed me and brought me peace. His perfect love cast away my fear. As I relaxed in His love, I heard quiet footsteps in the hallway. The door to the sanctuary opened. David. He walked toward me with sure steps—with confident steps—and I knew the Lord had ministered peace to him as well. He embraced me and gently wiped the tear stains from my face with sweet kisses.

I love my man.

We had endured a fierce battle. We both felt bruised, even abused, because the business meeting had been so vile. But you know what? Our God is able. Our God is faithful. And our God never left our side. Those truths keep me from going crazy. I know that *I know* my husband and I have been called to ministry. I'm learning that ministry is full of spiritual bloodshed most of us are not prepared for. Not exactly what we want to hear, is it? But it's true. When we step out as ministers of the gospel, all hell will break loose. When the Word of God is preached with power and boldness, the gates of hell will rattle.

You must have experienced something similar, or you wouldn't be reading this book. You're not alone. If you receive nothing else from this book, cling to this: You're not alone in your pain. You're not alone in your disillusionment, and you're not alone in your confusion about God's faithfulness to protect His children. You are not alone.

David and I walked arm-in-arm to the parsonage. Silence stood like a sentinel around us as God cloaked us with a quiet knowing only other pastors and their wives understand. No need for words. Our hearts understood completely.

The next day we considered our options. The leadership—aka deacon board—made it clear that our day of dismissal had arrived. The deacons wanted us to leave because their power and control had been diminished. Under David's leadership, Christ had reclaimed the small rural church. The deacons no longer called the shots, which enraged them, blinded them, to the things of God. But the people loved us and wanted us to stay.

David said, "Honey, we need to leave."

"But why? Why must we be the ones to leave? *Again?*"

"Because I've prayed most of the night, and I believe we've done all we can do here."

"But the people love us," I cried.

"Yes, that's true, but you know as well as I do that they're not going to stand up to the deacons. Their power is too entrenched here. The people don't want to offend, so rather than fight for their church, most of them will slip away to another place of worship. Others will complain in the background, but they won't confront the leadership. God is releasing us from this situation."

I trust my husband's wisdom, really I do. But I didn't want to leave a church family *again*. I didn't think I could do it. When God calls us to a church, we love with our whole hearts. We become family.

But I trusted my husband, and I trusted my God.

Let me interject something here: not all deacons are self-serving, power-hungry men. Not by a long shot. We've met many deacons who fulfilled their vows of servanthood with wisdom and humility. But, unfortunately, many people in church leadership positions have acquired a sense of entitlement. That may sound harsh, but in my experience, a troubled church is typically governed by a self-righteous, stiff-necked deacon board. They're the enemies a man of God battles. And it isn't pretty. When you're married to that man of God, the pain can be brutal.

The phone rang incessantly over the next few days. Shock waves traveled through the phone lines. Hugs showed up at our back door. However, the decision had been made: David and I had to leave. But where would we go? We had no home, no income, and no insurance—nothing but broken and defeated spirits. I plummeted to a pit deep within my soul. Occasionally, I mumbled the name of Jesus, more an act of desperation than of faith and victory. In my misery, though, I clung to the words God had spoken to me at the altar: *Run to Me and be safe. I am the Sovereign Lord, the Almighty God, and I have not forsaken you. I will make a way where there seems to be no way.* The battle within raged.

It wasn't the first time we had been forced to leave a church.

It was the fourth time.

I wondered if it would be the deal breaker.

CHAPTER TWO

THE REDEMPTIVE WORK
OF GOD'S PEOPLE

THE PHONE RANG. David picked it up.

"Thank you," my husband said. I raised my eyebrows and cocked my head as I looked squarely at him.

Who is it? I mouthed. David shushed me.

"Really?" David said. "Nan and I are at a loss. I can't even think straight."

I tugged on David's sleeve. *What?* I mouthed the word silently.

"Are you serious? Brother, you're an answer to my prayers. I didn't know what we were going to do. We have to be out of the parsonage in two weeks, and we have no place to go. Yes. Yes, of course we can meet you. Thank you so much."

"Honey," David said, "you're not going to believe this. That was Pastor Steve White from Restoration Baptist Church. He heard what happened to us."

"Goodness. News travels fast."

"I know. Pastor Steve said his church has an empty parsonage we can stay in rent free for as long as we need. He and his wife have their own home."

"You're kidding me."

"No, seriously. About six years ago, the church voted to keep the parsonage available for ministry purposes. Two other pastors and their families have stayed there. It's only five minutes from here."

David and I hugged each other and wept over the goodness of God.

Later that afternoon, we pulled into the driveway to find an older red brick, ranch-style house with a welcoming porch. A tremendous maple tree sheltered the front yard. Beyond the rural road stood the church. An enormous wooden cross graced the corner of the church property. In the evening hours, a spotlight shone on its rough-hewn logs, casting a glorious shadow of redemption across the church doors. In the coming weeks and months, I found great comfort in the shadow of that cross—a daily reminder that God had not forgotten us.

Pastor Steve arrived soon after we did. David and I introduced ourselves and followed him onto the porch. An old aluminum screen door greeted us. As the pastor unlocked the door, I noticed chipped paint around the doorframe. Dirt and leaves had gathered against the corners of the porch.

"I'm sorry," Pastor Steve said, "but the house has been empty for almost two years now. A house needs a family to be a home."

"My goodness," I said, "please don't worry about that." But inside I was cringing. The parsonage we were forced to leave was the nicest home we had ever lived in. It was meticulously manicured inside and out. And now? What was this *gift* God had given us? I put on my happy-girl mask, but inside, my heart ripped a little more, the dagger-like torment stabbed a little deeper.

The door creaked as Pastor Steve pushed it open. Cobwebs dangled their sticky threads throughout each room. Linoleum, the color of persimmons, spread its ugliness from room to room. Moisture in the bathroom had peeled away layers of paint to expose yet more linoleum, this time on the wall surrounding the tub.

Father, I cried deep inside my silent pain, *how much more? Is this the best You can do?* Sarcasm rattled obnoxiously through my devastation and pride.

Interrupted in the midst of my pity party, I heard Pastor Steve apologizing for the condition of the empty home again. I surprised myself by saying, "No. Please don't apologize. You don't understand. All we really need is shelter and love."

Truer words had never been spoken: "all we really need is shelter and love."

Over the next several weeks, I cried an ocean of tears. I wrestled with God. At times, I demanded revenge. At other times, I crumpled into a broken heap of rejection and disillusionment and willed myself to live and not die. In God's great mercy and grace, David found temporary employment at the local community college. The job gave him a reason to get up in the morning, and it put food on the table, but, honestly, there could be no denying the deep wound spreading its infection throughout my husband's spirit. He battled the relentless questions and accusations Satan cast his way—questions of purpose, questions of "calling," questions of "why?" Again. We both determined in our hearts that we were finished with the traditional church. Done. Too much pain there. Church politics and agendas made us both want to throw up. Our hearts grew colder by the day.

A few weeks later, Pastor Steve stopped by for a visit. "Just wanted to check on you folks," he said. "We're here if you need us, and we're praying for you."

"Thank you," we answered.

"Sure would love for you to visit the church. No pressure, though. We know you need time and space to heal."

"Steve," my husband said, "we're afraid to put our hearts out there again. We'll visit soon, though. I promise."

David and Pastor Steve walked out to the car together. Steve stretched his arm around David's shoulder. They both lowered their heads in conversation. I watched as God used another pastor to pour affirmation into my wounded and defeated husband. I felt a slight softening of my heart. *Oh, no you don't,* I rebuked myself. *Don't let your guard down. It hurts too much.*

When David came back inside, he seemed lighter. "I think we should visit the church this Sunday."

"I don't think I'm ready."

"I don't think we'll ever be *ready,*" David said, "but I do think it's time."

David was right, of course, but I would need an extra measure of grace to darken the doors of a church again. How sad.

Sunday morning came much earlier than I desired. I hit the snooze button on the alarm several times, attempting to delay the inevitable. Blue jays chattered outside our window as they flitted from branch to branch on the ancient oak beside the house. Beams of sunlight slipped past the curtains. It seemed that all of creation cheered for me that morning. I tried to respond with happiness—honestly. Normally, I loved Sunday mornings, but on that day, I faced the Lord's Day with dread.

I rolled out of bed and stumbled toward the coffeepot. While David showered and the coffee perked, I stared out the kitchen window. My gaze locked on the giant cross outside the church building. *God*, I pleaded, *melt my heart. Help me trust again. I'm afraid, Lord. So afraid.*

"Honey, are you okay?" David asked as he walked into the kitchen.

"Yeah. Just thinking."

My man wrapped his strong arms around me and held me. What was I thinking at that moment? *Thank You, Lord, that someone on this planet knows how ripped apart my heart is right now—how wounded and confused my spirit is.*

I can imagine how strongly you're relating to my words at this moment. Remember? I'm someone who knows. No hurt like that of a rejected pastor and his wife, is there? But notice what is happening here: David and I are going through the fire *together*. Each spouse must allow the other to experience any emotions that crop up—accept them without judgment or condemnation. Accept the raw emotions with an outpouring of grace that only the Lord can give. Create a safe place for you and your husband to blow up when you need to, to have a meltdown when the dam of tears can no longer hold back the pain. Allow each other to be real. And when the emotions roll in like a tidal wave, take the hand of your honey and, together, tread water and surf the wave until peace returns. It will return. But it takes time, grace, and a whole lot of love and acceptance.

David interrupted my thoughts. Looking deep into my glistening eyes, he spoke, "Darlin', we can do this. God is with us. He is for us and He wants to make us strong again."

"I know. I know," I said to reassure myself.

"Well, okay then. Let's do this thing. It's time to get ready."

Forty-five minutes later, David and I walked up the front steps of Restoration Baptist Church. I paused when I reached the top stair and confronted the giant red doors beckoning me to enter. I looked at David.

"You go first," I said.

"Chicken," he said, grinning.

"Yep. That's my story and I'm sticking to it."

My sweetie pushed the heavy door open and led the way into the church foyer, past the double doors, down the center aisle, three rows to the left. Aisle seats, no less. *I guess we have our pew established again,* I thought sarcastically. *It's strange to sit so far back.* I lowered my head and peered at my surroundings, trying hard to remain unnoticed. The church bulletin shook in my hands. My heart beat rapidly, screaming to be heard as it raced to protect itself against future hurt. David reached over and took my hand. He gently squeezed three times—our private signal for "I love you." I squeezed three times back.

The choir stood and began to sing, "A mighty fortress is our God, a bulwark never failing." *Yes, Lord. You're my fortress,* my heart whispered.

Then run to Me and be safe, the Spirit of God whispered back.

I sat a little straighter. I glanced at David and he winked at me. "Our helper He, amid the flood of mortal ills prevailing: For still our ancient foe doth seek to work us woe." *Goodness, the choir sounds nice this morning.* My body relaxed. A little.

"Would everyone please stand and greet your neighbor?" Pastor Steve asked.

I hugged David. Out of the corner of my eye, I saw movement. People were coming our way. Lots of people. *Oh, help me, Jesus.*

"Hi. We're so glad y'all are with us this morning" ... "How's the parsonage? I hope it suits your needs" ... "If you ever need anything, don't hesitate to ask. The church wants to help you" ... "We've been praying for you" ... "We're here for you. If you need to cry, we want you to cry. If you need to sit quietly, we want you to know that's okay with us. We want you to heal so you can once again do the work God has called you to do."

The people of God kept coming our way. Pastor Steve gave them all the time they needed to encourage us. With each handshake, with each hug, grace and strength poured into our broken places. I wiped a grateful tear from my eye. Glancing at David, I saw a smile. The hurt he harbored in his eyes subsided a little that day. I could tell he was thinking. Praying. I could tell Jesus was ministering deep within his spirit.

At the close of service, David and I walked hand-in-hand back to our timeworn, red brick house—*our* parsonage. I pushed open the creaking door and smiled at the persimmon-colored linoleum. I had never noticed the gold flecks mixed in with the garish orange. *That's a nice touch, Lord. Thank You,* my spirit whispered to the Lord. *Have I told You lately that I love You and that I love this old house?*

As I think back on those months of healing, I realize that the Most High God—our Deliverer and Healer—knew exactly what we needed. That humble home was immersed in peace. It quickly became a safe haven against the works of the enemy. It became a place of healing and rest, the rest of God. In that humble sanctuary, God began to, once again, knit our hearts together with the hearts of His people.

Once again, we learned to trust. Slowly, at first. Surely, at last.

God wants to do the same for you. There is fellowship in His suffering—an intimacy that can't be obtained otherwise. In the following chapters, I pray that God will bring you to a place of healing—a place where you'll never be the same because of His amazing grace. I pray that you'll find Him faithful and that you'll learn to trust again.

CHAPTER THREE

HERE I AM, LORD. SEND ... ME?

The Peril of Meeting Expectations

THE SUMMER OF 1988 took us to Tulsa, Oklahoma, for a college recruitment weekend hosted by Oral Roberts University's School of Theology and Missions. *Could this be the seminary we'd been looking for?*

Before we left home, and throughout each day of our trip, I had been asking—begging—God to confirm our steps. We were an east coast family. Our small children were growing up surrounded by grandmas and grandpas, aunts and uncles, cousins ... you get the picture. Telling our families God had called us into ministry was one thing. But taking their grandbabies halfway across America was a whole different story.

Intuitively, I knew obstacles, criticisms, and doubt would be hurled in our direction. I boldly asked God to show us beyond any shadow of doubt that He had, indeed, called us to the seminary at ORU. In Tulsa. Fifteen hundred miles from home. I wanted more than a good feeling that weekend; I needed something to stand on. I needed something I could hold up as a shield when the opposition came.

We arrived in Tulsa on a balmy Friday afternoon and were quickly immersed in seminary life. Everything about the weekend felt right. We were impressed with the School of Theology. David and I were in agreement about everything the seminary stood for, but I still wanted something more for my confirmation, and I didn't hesitate to remind the Lord of that.

Chapel was scheduled for Sunday morning. Afterward, we would board the plane for South Carolina. Time was running out. We dressed for the service. I fumbled around packing our belongings, totally distracted. This thing— this calling—was huge. I firmly believed that David and I had heard the Lord correctly, but our family? I couldn't get past the dread of telling them we'd soon be packing up— grandbabies and all—and moving to Tulsa. Once again, I prayed, *Lord, everything about ORU feels right, but I can't base this decision on what "feels right." I need to know that I know this is what You want us to do.*

David took my hand, and we hurried over to the auditorium. It was packed with four hundred other prospective students. We found an aisle seat on the fifteenth row. I looked around at the hopeful, eager faces wanting to hear from God. I thought my heart was going to beat out of my chest with anticipation. Time was short. Within a couple of hours, we would board a plane to Charleston. I needed confirmation—something tangible—I could take back home. The preacher spoke boldly from God's Word. He charged us to walk in obedience to God's call. As before, everything *felt* so right. But "so right" wasn't what I needed. *Lord,* I prayed, *please. I need something more than feelings.*

At that moment—no, I'm not kidding—the preacher stopped mid-sentence. He crossed the stage, walked down four steps and strode up the aisle in our direction. I set my jaw so my mouth wouldn't fly open as I watched him. He walked with determination, as if on a mission. When he got to the fifteenth row, he stopped. Pointing directly at David, he said, "You, sir, are a leader, and you are called to preach God's Word."

Whoa! I think that will do the trick, Lord. Honestly, I almost fell out of my seat. All along, I had been praying expectant prayers, but when God answered in such a profound way, I almost fainted.

Please know, not everyone has such a dramatic confirmation of God's calling. Remember? He often speaks in a delicate, whispering voice.

David and I were engaged when the Spirit of God first stirred within him. He lay on his bed reading the Word, seeking God. Isaiah 61:1 leapt off the page: *The Spirit of the LORD God is upon Me, because the LORD has anointed Me to preach good tidings to the poor; He has sent Me to heal the brokenhearted, to proclaim liberty to the captives, and the opening of the prison to those who are bound.* No fireworks burst in the sky; no band of angels sang at the foot of his bed. It was only Jesus and David. But it was *oh so real.*

As for my calling, I was seeking the Lord about our upcoming marriage. I knelt by my bed. Praise flowed from my lips as I thanked the Lord for such a wonderful man. Out of the blue, the Spirit of the Lord began to whisper in my spirit. He told me David would be my teammate—we would be His servants—to take His love and security into a hurting world. The moment was very quiet, but I knew that I knew I had heard from the Lord. In fact, I wrote the entire message in my Bible and dated it July 13, 1982. The call was that profound.

Oftentimes, the husband is confident in his calling to pastoral ministry, but the wife is stumbling behind him, trying to keep up, trying to find her place. She may be ecstatic about the possibilities. She may be humbled by the responsibilities and apprehensive about the requirements. Or, she may be angry and resentful that God would require such a thing as this—this calling for her husband. This wife typically wants nothing to do with it.

Would you mind if we talk about that? We're called to stand by our husband's side because we're one with him in marriage; therefore, the shadow of his calling falls upon us. If you're a pastor's wife who finds herself thrust into ministry kicking and screaming, I encourage you to take a moment and allow your thoughts to refocus. Rather than seeing yourself tied to this invasive monster named ministry because you happened to fall in love with a man after God's heart, open your eyes to see the face of Jesus.

Do you see Him? Take my hand. Let's walk together.

In my mind, Jesus is sitting on a boulder in the center of a lush pasture. A brilliant aura surrounds Him. His eyes are fixed on us, willing us to come and sit with Him awhile. We cozy up to Him and lean against His legs—me on one side, you on the other. A gentle breeze whips His linen robe about us. The warmth of the noonday sun feels good against our faces. Both of us turn our eyes to behold our Savior. Astonishing love emanates through His gaze. He sees your tears and gently reaches over to wipe them from your cheek. Jesus addresses your fear, your resentment, your feelings of inadequacy—not with words, but through the remarkable power of His Spirit. Do you sense His Presence? Friend, you're loved by an amazing God. The fact that He has entrusted you to undergird your husband speaks highly of His trust in you. He has equipped you with the strengths your husband lacks. He has joined you to your husband for eternal purposes that you may not see at this time, but they're divine, nevertheless. This is a holy calling.

In Paul's letter to Timothy, he exhorts the young disciple of Christ to be faithful in the face of struggles and hardships for the sake of the gospel: *[God] has saved us and called us with a holy calling, not according to our works, but according to His own purpose and grace which was given to us in Christ Jesus before time began* (2 Timothy 1:9). Just as Timothy was called alongside the apostle Paul for the sake of the gospel, you're called alongside your husband. God has a plan. God has a purpose. Recognition of these eternal purposes is the beginning of a beautiful love story between you, your honey, and the Lord Most High. It doesn't get much better than this. But we must open our eyes to see, and we must open our hearts to the needs of our Savior and the needs of our husbands.

Have you ever considered what your life would be like without Jesus—without His love and grace? Do you remember the moment you first heard the marvelous news of His salvation? Maybe it was through the spoken word of a preacher gripping the edges of his pulpit, proclaiming the strong Word of God. Maybe. But chances are you first opened your heart to receive Jesus through the testimony of a sister, a friend, or through the acceptance of a camp counselor. You possibly heard the Good News of Jesus Christ through a total stranger who reached out to you as you sat crying on a lonely park bench. God's messengers come in all sizes, all colors, and all ages—male and female. We're all called to the ministry of reconciliation. Consider what the apostle Paul spoke to the church at Corinth:

Now all things are of God, who has reconciled us to Himself through Jesus Christ, and has given us the ministry of reconciliation, that is, that God was in Christ reconciling the world to Himself, not imputing their trespasses to them, and has committed to us the word of reconciliation. Now then, we are ambassadors for Christ, as though God were pleading through us: we implore you on Christ's behalf, be reconciled to God.
(2 Corinthians 5:18-20)

Reflect on this: We're *all* called. We're *all* ambassadors for Christ, as though God were pleading through us. Isn't that amazing? As pastors' wives, we have the privilege of holding our honey's hand as we answer this call.

I can still remember the moment I realized that God wanted to use me to help build His kingdom on earth. This was long before David came on the scene. In fact, I was very young in the Lord. I was in college, attending a campus Bible study. The lesson that particular night zeroed in on these same verses from 2 Corinthians. Gaining an understanding of this godly principle worked wonders in my spirit. In those days, I had no self-esteem; I shied away from everything and everyone. I was a mess on the inside. But I discovered Jesus loved me anyway. In fact, He loved me in spite of me. And then I realized that He wanted to use me as a minister of reconciliation—He wanted to use me to bring others to the foot of the cross. *Me.* Oh my goodness. That knowledge set me free.

It can set you free also so you can know in your *knower* that God Himself has called you. He sees in you what you don't see in yourself. He sees goodness and faithfulness. He sees humility and grace. He sees a beautiful woman whom He needs to complete the ministry of her husband. God has a plan. He *always* has a plan.

Are you beginning to feel more secure in your role? Maybe you're thinking, *if she only knew!* I do know. And so does every other pastor's wife. Remember? You are not alone. And guess who else knows your doubts and fears? Your Father God. Please allow the following Scripture to fill you to overflowing with strength for this journey: *For in Him dwells all the fullness of the Godhead bodily; and you are complete in Him, who is the head of all principality and power* (Colossians 2:9-10). You are complete in Him— in Jesus. We've been given the fullness of God through

Christ. Jesus said to Philip, *"He who has seen me has seen the Father"* (John 14:9). Jesus was God with skin on. There is no part of God that isn't expressed in Jesus. So if we have the fullness of Christ within us, we have everything God has and is.

When your doubts assail you, think on these things. Awaken your heart to hear the voice of the Lord imploring you to be His ambassador. You have been chosen. You have nothing to prove to anyone. Walk in the knowledge that God completely approves of you and dwells richly within you. Once you recognize who has called you and for what purpose, you'll realize you don't need to play to the applause of anyone or anything else. You live only to receive the affirmation of Your Father who loved you before you even knew Him. His pleasure and embrace will override the battles that ensue.

That's where the sweet love story I mentioned earlier comes in. Remember? The one between you, your honey, and Jesus. Can you imagine joining hands with the One who made you because He chose you and your husband to take His love to a hurting world? Can you wrap your mind around the intimacy of the relationship your union with Him creates—to be coworkers with the Son of God? Oh my goodness. That makes it all worthwhile.

Let's take a look at the beautiful, fulfilling side of the calling. This is the side where goose bumps reside—the side that causes your spirit to soar and cry out to Jesus in gratitude. Even when David and I have moments where we conclude we're done, that we've had enough, Jesus whispers to us through lives that have been touched. Many stories come to mind, but one stands out as a reminder of why we continue to say yes to ministry.

The frigid January day generated frosty breath and hopes for snow. Several of us loaded up the church van with boxes of donated winter coats, gloves, and socks along with handmade scarves. Full of anticipation, we made our trek to the local soup kitchen. Our group had said yes to the burden the Lord placed on us for the homeless in our area. We were excited to be used by Him.

We unloaded the van in front of the facility. Abandoned buildings stood as shadows of days gone by. Railroad tracks crisscrossed the industrial neighborhood; grime and trash littered the streets. But still we smiled. We knew Jesus had called us to this moment, and He was with us. People began to amble in for a nutritious lunch. Men, women, and children came. The elderly hobbled to the front door. Faces were downcast; body language spoke of defeat. But then, like a burst of sunshine through the billowing clouds of a storm, the precious eyes of these homeless folks lit up when they saw the coats and accessories. Our timidity fled as God's love overflowed into the lives of society's unlovely members.

And then she rounded the corner of the building.

Her camouflage jacket was tattered and caked with patches of mud. Strands of stringy blonde hair dangled over her piercing blue eyes, daring the world to approach.

"What's your name?" I asked.

"Mary," she muttered.

The stench stung my nostrils as God filled me with compassion for this lost soul. Mary was living in a cardboard box beneath a nearby overpass. She was cold, tired, and nearly destroyed by the painful turn her life had taken. Gently, I persuaded her to look at me.

"Mary, you're precious to God. He is with you and wants to help you." Lifeless eyes stared back at me in disbelief. "You're cold. Here, please take my coat." This fragile woman nodded, eyes darting back and forth. "May I hug you?"

Again she nodded.

I held her in my arms, willing the walls to fall down. She remained silent, but then I felt it. A warm tear trickled from her cheek to mine. I hugged her again.

"Thank you," she whispered.

I motioned for David to join us. Together we held this hurting woman. We allowed her to wring out the pain through a flood of tears. As her sobs turned to deep breaths, we began to pray over her. We asked the Lord to restore her life, to replace her despair with His glorious hope for a better tomorrow. The three of us basked in the light of His love, oblivious to the others around us.

Mary lifted her head and looked deep into David's eyes. "I don't know Jesus, but I want to. Please, can you tell me about Him?"

Oh my goodness. There, surrounded by concrete and littered streets, God gave us the gift of a lost soul. A touch from heaven. A servant's reward.

It was awesome.

My sister, may I pray for you?

Father God, You are the Almighty God, Maker of heaven and earth. Your ways are higher than our ways; Your thoughts are above the activity of the earth. You, Lord, are bathed in the light of eternity, and we walk in Your shadow to fulfill Your purposes. I bring my precious sister before Your throne of grace. As she bows before You, Lord, I ask that You touch her with a fresh anointing for the work You have called her to. Stir up a passion within this daughter of Yours to share Your love with those around her. Kindle afresh the love she has for her husband. I ask that Your perfect love would cast away all fear and dread she may be experiencing. I ask that You pour out Your amazing grace on her, her work, her marriage, and her ministry. Put a spring in her step, Lord. Cause her to laugh at life's absurdities. Awaken the eyes of her heart to understand that You have chosen her to undergird her husband—to understand that You have chosen her to do a work that only she can fulfill. Anoint her with boldness, wisdom, and extraordinary love. Help her walk in compassion as she looks at the world through Your eyes.

Thank You, Lord. You are Wonderful, Counselor, the Mighty God, and the Prince of Peace, and yet You know each of us by name. What a blessed assurance this knowledge brings. We want to serve You, Lord, with our whole hearts. Bless You, Father. We praise You, for You alone are worthy of our praise. In Jesus' name I pray, amen.

Promises for the Peril of Meeting Expectations

God said, *"Before I formed you in the womb I knew you,*
before you were born I set you apart;
I appointed you as a prophet to the nations."
~ Jeremiah 1:5 (NIV)

And the teachers and those who are wise
shall shine like the brightness of the firmament,
and those who turn many to righteousness
(to uprightness and right standing with God)
[shall give forth light] like the stars forever and ever.
~ Daniel 12:3 (AMP)

But also for this very reason, giving all diligence,
add to your faith virtue, to virtue knowledge,
to knowledge self-control, to self-control perseverance,
to perseverance godliness, to godliness brotherly kindness,
and to brotherly kindness love.
For if these things are yours and abound,
you will be neither barren nor unfruitful
in the knowledge of our Lord Jesus Christ ...
Therefore, brethren, be even more diligent
to make your call and election sure,
for if you do these things you will never stumble.
~ 2 Peter 1:5-7, 10

CHAPTER FOUR

THE FELLOWSHIP
OF HIS SUFFERINGS

The Peril of Rose-Colored Glasses

MY GRANDMOTHER LOVED birds. She painted pictures of birds. She collected bird figurines and fine dishes from the Audubon Society. Her flower garden was alive with chatter and bursts of color swooping from branch to branch. I share this love with her.

Upon Grandmother's death, I received a porcelain figurine of a bluebird perched on a dogwood branch. This too had come from the Audubon Society many years ago. Not only was it pleasant to my eye, but also its beauty connected me to my grandmother's heart. No dollar amount could ever replace the joy this little guy brought me.

My boys were ages three and four. Wrestling Mania was big at our house—at least the Jones brothers' version.

They giggled and tumbled, somersaulting with legs thrashing. Whoops of joy pinged through the house.

And then it happened.

A flailing leg got too close to the coffee table and slammed into the bluebird. Wings shattered. Hearts broke.

"Mommy, Mommy! We're sorry. We're so sorry, Mommy."

I felt sick, but the remorse from my boys kept me tethered to sanity.

"It's okay. I'll find a way to fix it. It's okay."

Oh Lord, how am I going to repair this damage? It will never be the same.

I remembered the superglue in the kitchen cabinet. *Maybe, just maybe.* I gathered the fractured bird and carefully carried the pieces to the kitchen table. Piece by broken piece, I molded the bluebird back to its former beauty. The lines of fragmentation were visible if examined closely, but the superglue did the trick. Bonded. Restored. Complete.

Fellowship is like that.

The Greek word for "fellowship" is *koinonia* (koy-nohn-ee-ah) and means sharing, unity, partnership. It denotes an intimate bond. *"Koinonia* cements the believers to the Lord Jesus and to each other."[2] Imagine being so bonded to the Lord that nothing can separate you from Him. Consider also that in the bonding you find restoration and completeness.

So what happens to this fellowship when suffering is involved? The Bible clearly refers to the *fellowship* of Jesus' sufferings, so there must be something to this odd paradox. I believe God wants us to draw strength from recognizing the bond that is secured through the fellowship of His sufferings. He wants us to soak up this truth like a dry sponge and gain strength for the journey. Let's begin with the apostle Paul:

> *Yet indeed I also count all things loss for the excellence of the knowledge of Christ Jesus my Lord, for whom I have suffered the loss of all things, and count them as rubbish, that I may gain Christ and be found in Him, not having my own righteousness, which is from the law, but that which is through faith in Christ, the righteousness which is from God by faith; that I may know Him and the power of His resurrection, and the fellowship of His sufferings, being conformed to His death, if, by any means, I may attain to the resurrection from the dead.* (Philippians 3:8-11)

First and foremost, Paul proclaims that he has been *found* in Jesus—his eyes have been opened (literally) to see the truth of the saving grace of Jesus Christ. No longer will man obtain righteousness through the practice of religious laws. Paul belongs to Jesus. He has given himself wholly to his Savior. Paul now walks in the knowledge that righteousness comes through a living faith in Jesus Christ.

As Christians, we too have been found in Jesus.

The apostle Paul is writing this letter to the Church at Philippi from prison. Paul—a man's man, a Jew to the Jew, a zealous Pharisee who was highly esteemed for his intensive persecution of the followers of Jesus—sits in a filthy prison cell, shackled, hungry, and alone. Why? Paul loves Jesus and works hard to build the Kingdom of God. Although he has sacrificed almost everything for the sake of the gospel, Paul believes he has, in fact, gained all things because he has been found *in* Christ. Imagine that. How could Paul possibly believe that he has gained everything when he lives in poverty, is beaten on a regular basis, and is held captive in a Roman prison?

Paul isn't a criminal. He loves Jesus.

Does that sound like justice? Does that sound like Paul is serving a powerful, loving God? How can we, as pastors' wives, experience this same joy of gaining everything in the face of great loss? What happens when we've been kicked out of the parsonage and stabbed in the back because we love and serve Jesus? Does *that* sound like justice? Does it sound like we're serving a powerful, loving God? I've wrestled with these questions more than once. And God has opened my eyes.

Let's dig a little deeper, taking another glimpse at Paul's heart: *Yet indeed I also count all things loss ... that I may know Him and the power of His resurrection (eternal life), and the fellowship of His sufferings.* That I may know Him. Paul realizes there is no greater joy than knowing Jesus intimately. No greater fulfillment. Honestly, that seems obvious, doesn't it? But here's what I'm learning: in this passage, the Greek word for "know" is *ginosko* and in Hebrew it's *yada*. They're virtually interchangeable. Paul is saying that to know Jesus in this way—*ginosko*—refers to an intimate relationship. It involves the heart. *Ginosko* isn't gained by standing back and observing. *Ginosko* comes through active, intentional engagement with one another.

Not only do we know Him, but He also knows us. The relationship is so intimate that we begin to take on His characteristics.

At the time of this writing, David and I have been married for thirty-one years. He's hysterically funny and keeps me in stitches most of the time, except for those moments I want to kill him. Just sayin'. The longer we're together, the more alike we become. I know what he's thinking in almost every situation. I know his expectations, his dreams. I know how David will react at any given time. Many times when the phone rings, I'll know it's David before I pick up the phone. That's how close we are. And that's because I *ginosko* him.

Let's look at *ginosko* another way. David's father, Lee Jones, was a remarkable man of faith. His spirit was so tender to the things of God. David is like his father in many ways, even in the silly things. Pappy (my affectionate name for his dad) loved to sing and whistle. When something was on his mind or he was troubled by something, he would sing, "Dee, dee, dee" in a random tune. David does the same thing. He takes on the characteristics of his father because he *ginoskos* him. Here's another example: Our grandson, Jamison, adores his father, David Jr. They're inseparable. Although Jamison's still very young, it's clear who his father is. Jamison looks like his daddy. He talks like his daddy. He loves the things his daddy loves, and he even walks like his dad. How crazy is that? And *why* is that? Because they *ginosko* one another. Their love for one another is complete. Their relationship is intimate and rich. To the observer, there is no doubt these two belong to each other.

"*Ginosko* is to know to the degree that it will reproduce itself in the same likeness and image of that which is known. When we truly know Jesus, He'll reproduce His likeness and image in our lives. Therefore, to truly know Jesus is to be like Him—to bear His image."³ Knowing Jesus in such a deep, personal manner changes our lives. And guess how this happens. Yep! Through the fellowship of His suffering. I know, right? But we must look at the reward. Is there any greater gift on earth than that of knowing (*ginosko*) Christ?

Again, the words of Paul: *Yet indeed I also count all things loss ... that I may know Him and the power of His resurrection* [eternal life], *and the fellowship of His sufferings.* Paul desired to be identified with Jesus in all things, not only the lovely and privileged things of this world, but also those things that are abased. I love the way *The Amplified Bible* expresses these verses:

> [*For my determined purpose is*] *that I may know Him* [*that I may progressively become more deeply and intimately acquainted with Him, perceiving and recognizing and understanding the wonders of His Person more strongly and more clearly*], *and that I may in that same way come to know the power outflowing from His resurrection* [*which it exerts over believers*], *and that I may so share His sufferings as to be continually transformed* [*in spirit into His likeness even*] *to His death,* [*in the hope*] *that if possible I may attain to the* [*spiritual and moral*] *resurrection* [*that lifts me*] *out from among the dead* [*even while in the body*].

Isn't that powerful?

> [Paul] did not desire merely to share his honors and triumphs in heaven, but, regarding his whole work as glorious, he wished to be wholly conformed to that, and, as far as possible, to be just like Christ. Many are willing to reign with Christ, but they would not be willing to suffer with him; many would be willing to wear a crown of glory like him, but not the crown of thorns; many would be willing to put on the robes of splendor which will be worn in heaven, but not the scarlet robe of contempt and mockery. They would desire to share the glories and triumphs of redemption, but not its poverty, contempt, and persecution. This was not the feeling of Paul. He wished in all things to be just like Christ, and hence he counted it an honor to be permitted to suffer as he did.[4]

Paul understood the beauty of sanctification. After all, isn't that what we're really talking about here? Becoming more Christ-like so that we might dwell with Him richly? That we might *know* Him and the fullness of His glory? To be set apart for God? Sharing in His suffering for the sake of righteousness purifies us and molds us into a vessel that can be filled to the brim with the Holy Spirit and then poured out upon a hurting and dying world.

Embrace these powerful words: *Behold, I have refined you, but not as silver; I have tried and chosen you in the furnace of affliction* (Isaiah 48:10 AMP). Affliction. Suffering, pain, grief, misery, distress—sound familiar?

Ask the Lord to open the eyes of your heart to see and understand the compelling image I'm going to paint for you:

The silversmith wiped the sweat from his brow with the back of his calloused hand. The flames leaped in the bowels of the furnace, licking the air for oxygen, preparing to devour anything not pure enough to withstand its sweltering fury. Carefully, the old gentleman filled his stone "smithing" bowl with slivers and filings of discarded silver—throwaways deliberately chosen for the vessel he would craft. He placed them "just so" into the bowl and then eased it into the center of the flames where the heat was greatest. This was necessary to burn away anything impure. Only the finest silver would do for the vessel the Master silversmith would shape after the refining fire.

The old man reached for his chair. His fingers, black with soot, grasped the chair's carved back and pulled it closer to the furnace. He sat down, never taking his eyes off the silver that was now beginning to melt and swirl in the inferno. The silversmith knew the exact moment to remove the silver—a second too long, and it would be destroyed.

He kept a careful eye—watching, waiting—looking for that moment when the impurities were gone.

At last, the dross pulled away from the silver. The silversmith eased the stone bowl out of the flames. He peered into the liquid luster. Reflected back to him, as in a mirror, was his own image. The old gentleman knew the refining fire had completed its work. The silver was pure. It shone with the brightness of the morning star. It reflected its Master's image. Now the vessel for which it was intended could be shaped and molded by the Master's hand.

Are you in the throes of suffering now? Is the anguish of your heart threatening to suffocate you? The Master knows. He keeps a careful watch over you, governing the trial and adjusting the flame so you won't be eternally marred or destroyed by its pain.

The Lord is honored by your willingness to endure this trial by fire for the sake of His Kingdom. His eyes are on you. His eyes are on me. I find great comfort in that knowledge. And, because David and I have suffered on behalf of the gospel, God's Kingdom on earth has been advanced. That also comforts me. You, my friend, can say the same. We're bonded to Christ because we've suffered for Him. Could there be any greater honor on earth than to be used by God to bring the saving knowledge of Jesus—the extraordinary love of God—to a broken soul? I think not.

Do you remember your first pastorate? Perhaps you and your husband anticipated your assignment with sheer bliss and rose-colored glasses. Excitement filled your heart. Dreams of lives changed and communities set on fire for God filled your mind. And you knew you were going to be used by God in joyous, peaceful, holy ways.

A pastor and his wife usually enter ministry with much naiveté. We think our eyes are wide open. Certainly our hearts are opened wide. We enter ministry with a heart that wants to be used by God. That's a wonderful thing. What we don't realize is that ministry places us on the front line of battle. Many, many times our rose-colored glasses get shattered. Unless we open our eyes to see God's eternal purposes in all things, we may walk away feeling defeated and totally confused about our calling.

Our first pastorate was near the east coast of North Carolina. Our church sat alongside a rural highway surrounded by wheat fields and peanut farmers. This rural area hadn't advanced far beyond the racial issues of the 1960s. Prejudice abounded. Even seating in local restaurants remained segregated—in the early 1990s! We were amazed. The local schools were a mess. Dropout rates climbed each year; school discipline was virtually nonexistent. Let's just say, the area was ripe for harvest.

This small church displayed an astounding attribute, quite amazing for the area: African-Americans, Caucasians, and Hispanics worshiped together as the Body of Christ. Talk about a light in the darkness. Wow!

Because the schools in the area were so horrible, the church answered the call to incorporate a Christian school into its facilities. Sounds like a great idea, right? Wrong. After several years, the school began to dominate the church. Instead of being a church with a school, it began functioning as a school with a church. By that, I mean the needs of the school were met before the needs of the church—without the congregation's approval or knowledge. This happened because most of the student body was comprised of the deacons' children and grandchildren. The wife of one of the deacons served as the church treasurer. Ahem!

Long before David and I arrived, a core group of church members began praying that God would correct the problem. They felt their hands were tied because the problem was rooted in the church leadership. Period. Little did we know that we were about to enter a hornet's nest. We arrived blowing our trumpets and stylin' our rose-colored glasses. We had no idea what we were about to encounter. We had no idea that we were the answer to the prayers of people begging God to bring correction to their church. Can anyone say, here comes the cavalry?

Everything was progressing beautifully in the beginning. New visitors warmed the pews each Sunday. Salvations and baptisms were a common exclamation point to our worship services. The church was growing both physically and spiritually. David and I were in heaven, or so we thought. At least, that was the view from our rose-colored glasses.

One Sunday, a church member serving on the events committee requested permission to order more plates and cups for an upcoming covered-dish dinner. The treasurer immediately vetoed the request, stating the kitchen budget had no available funds. *What? The sanctuary has been full for months.* Red flags flew high that day. David looked at me with raised eyebrows. I began to pray. We both knew the budget should have contained ample funds to keep the kitchen stocked. So did the congregation. No one challenged the treasurer at that moment, but that was the beginning of the exposure of a dirty little secret.

David began questioning church members about the mysterious reduction in church funds. (He waited to talk with the treasurer until he had more information.) What he found out was alarming. He discovered that for several years, only the school—never the church—had the funds necessary to move forward. He discovered that when the church voted against funding something for the school, the piece of equipment, or whatever, was purchased anyway. The core group of prayer warriors was aware of this, but they didn't know what to do about it except to pray that God would bring someone to correct the problem. They realized God's hand of blessing would be removed unless this sin, a potentially illegal activity, was stopped.

David continued to gather information from reliable sources. At the next deacon meeting, he put it on the table: "It has come to my attention that church monies are being spent against the will of the church in order to keep the school alive. It has also come to my attention that the church books are being laundered in a way that covers up this deceptive behavior."

The deacons went into denial mode—angrily. But remember, their children and grandchildren were the bulk of the student body at the school. And the treasurer was a deacon's wife. And they were in this together. Ruffled feathers is an understatement. Their deceit and dishonesty had been exposed. David offered them a week to pray and search their hearts about what God would have them do. He hoped they would confess their sin so the situation could be resolved and God's glory returned to the church body.

That didn't happen.

By the next day, the telephone "ministry" had begun. The deacons' wives were stirring the pot big-time. Their argument was that the church had only known David and me for about a year, whereas the congregation had known the deacon board for almost ten years. They argued that David was lying. Many people fell for it. Things got very ugly. Fast.

We began receiving obscene phone calls. David's name was ripped from the church sign. We were ordered out of the parsonage. All this because David stood for righteousness. *Really, God?*

But I married a wise man.

A large group of church members stood with us and appreciated David's efforts to make the necessary changes. We learned that two other pastors before David had discovered the misappropriation of funds, but rather than deal with it, they resigned and hightailed it out of there. The second one actually challenged the leadership at a deacons' meeting and was pushed against a wall. No kidding. After that, he left.

David contacted his supervisor, the Director of Missions (DOM), and asked for guidance. He knew something had to be done. This precious church belonged to God, not to the folks who had abused their power. Our DOM recommended that a team of mediators from our denomination come and conduct a business meeting, which would expose the problem. David agreed. A few days later, our DOM called and asked David if he still wanted to hold the meeting. David asked him if there was any other way to bring correction. He was told no.

David said, "If this is what it takes to place this church back in God's hands, then I'm willing."

The DOM replied, "Then be prepared. They're out for blood."

I couldn't believe it was happening. *This is what it means to be a minister of the gospel? Are you kidding me, Lord?* Many people were praying for us and for our church. As the meeting approached, the battle intensified. David and I prayed in earnest. We sought God's wisdom, His comfort, and especially His courage. God spoke to us through His Word: *He was oppressed and He was afflicted, yet He opened not His mouth; He was led as a lamb to the slaughter, and as a sheep before its shearers is silent, so He opened not His mouth* (Isaiah 53:7). Although this is a prophetic verse about Jesus, we knew it was the Lord's instruction for us. We were to be silent before our accusers and let God defend us.

On the night of the meeting, people began to fill the sanctuary while others mingled in the foyer. David and I waited in his office with a few close friends. We stormed the gates of heaven while we waited for the meeting to begin. About ten minutes before seven, we walked into the sanctuary from a side door. I thought I was going to die. Piercing stares felt like knives penetrating my soul. I could hear whispers all around us. And then the meeting was called to order.

Everyone was asked to stand for an opening prayer. As I stood, I began to feel woozy. The room was spinning. My knees turned to rubber. David and a dear friend grabbed my elbows and held me until the fainting spell passed. My rose-colored glasses lay in broken pieces all about me. My spirit shattered. My mind swirled with painful thoughts. *How could this be happening?*

Our Director of Missions led the congregation in a vote to accept the authority, decisions, and recommendations of the mediating board. For about an hour, the deacons ranted about David's gall to accuse them of misappropriation of funds while supportive church members countered the attack. The treasurer was called into question. She hemmed and hawed and squirmed her way out of the fire. But David had gathered evidence of her book laundering. The stench of evil permeated the air. A young woman began throwing up. People cried. People shouted.

David and I sat quietly.

Then the question came.

"Pastor David, do you have anything to say in your defense?" asked the mediator.

David looked deep into my eyes and then turned his attention to the man in charge. "No sir. I have nothing to say. My God will defend me."

David took my hand and squeezed it three times. "I love you too," I squeezed back.

The meeting was adjourned for a thirty-minute recess while the board of mediators discussed the situation. Our DOM and a few close friends surrounded us with their protective love. Reverend Kelly, the DOM, told us that in his twenty-six years of ministry, he had never experienced such evil in a room. Can you imagine? I didn't realize it then, but I do now: a spiritual war was going on in the heavens for this precious church and its faithful few. Being aware of the reality of spiritual warfare will help you find purpose in your suffering too.

The mediation board called David into their meeting room. "Brother David, we believe you're being completely honest with us, and for that we thank you. This is a serious situation. We're going to recommend that the church remove all those in positions of authority and start from scratch. We also will recommend that the members hold an election to replace all of the deacons and clerks, as well as the treasurer. We recommend that you stay in place as pastor, but, you must know, we're concerned for your safety. How do you feel about this?"

"I want to do what's best for the church," David said.

"We honestly think you and Nan will be in danger if you stay. We have never seen anything quite like this. But we'll recommend that you remain as pastor if that is what you want."

David asked them if we could have a few minutes to talk and pray about our decision. We walked to David's office in silence, thoughts swirling. We knelt right there on that cold, hardwood floor and poured out our hearts before the Lord. I laid my head on David's chest while he held me, and we waited for an answer. Then the Lord whispered to us:

I have called you, My children, to build, but not like you think. My ways are higher than your ways; My thoughts are not your thoughts. I have called you to build the foundation strong—to shore it up. The foundation is a good foundation, but it is not strong in everyone. I have sent you to make the foundation sure and strong. You will repair the breaches. The breaches need repair, for they are broken. Fix your eyes on Me and I will lead you. You have done your work here. Go forth and I will lead you with My hand upon you.

David and I walked down the hall to the mediation board. David told them that we had decided our work here was over and that God was leading us elsewhere. David and I slipped out a back door while the mediation board presented their findings to the church body. As you can imagine, the deacons were outraged that David was found innocent. They were also furious to learn that the recommendation was to take the church back to ground zero and reelect officers of the church and a new deacon board. The church, especially after seeing the deacons' behavior, accepted the recommendation. Most of the deacons stormed out, never to return. Over the next few weeks, with the care and guidance of the DOM, new leadership was put into place, and a pulpit-search committee was formed.

Now, fast-forward about three years.

God gave us our hearts' desires and moved us back home to the mountains of North Carolina. David received a letter from Brother Kelly giving us an update on the church. The report was good. A new pastor had been in place for a while. The school was closed. A new deacon board was serving in a godly manner, along with other officers of the church. In the letter, Brother Kelly asked David if he could give them our contact information. The church body had something they wanted to say to us. David agreed.

Over the next few weeks, we received letters asking for our forgiveness. The first letter to arrive was from the congregation at large. They apologized for what had happened, stating that the Lord had revealed the truth to them as a church body. They believed they needed our forgiveness in order for the church to move forward with God's blessing and grace. We were floored. Humbled. Blessed. Tears of joy and gratitude coursed down our cheeks. Then we started receiving individual letters from church members requesting the same. The people seemed mortified that they had been so easily deceived. Their sweet words affirmed our calling and helped to heal our wounded spirits.

We found it easy to offer forgiveness. I believe you will also. You'll find God's grace is sufficient. You'll find a new appreciation for how easily people can be deceived and enter into the mire, yourself included. And you'll recognize that the Hand of God is upon you, working His will and His way through you, His servant, to accomplish the building of His Kingdom. *For to you it has been granted* on behalf of Christ, not only to believe in Him, but also to suffer for His sake (Philippians 1:29).

I'm asking you to pick up your shattered rose-colored glasses and present them as an offering to the Lord. I still have some superglue in my kitchen cabinet. You're more than welcome to borrow it.

Let's pray.

Father God, together my sister and I bring our broken dreams, our bleeding hearts, and our shattered images of a perfect life of ministry to You. It's so hard to move forward after the abuse, the lies, and the deception. But, Lord, we choose to move forward because of You. Because we love You. Because You ask this of us. We choose You, Jesus. Bind us to You intimately. Make Yourself known to us in deeper ways. Open the eyes of our hearts to understand Your eternal purposes. Help us heal, Lord. Help us to trust once again with a renewed vision of what You have called us to. Thank You, Lord. You are a mighty God. We love You, Lord. In Jesus' name I pray, amen.

Promises for the Peril of Rose-Colored Glasses

We are hard-pressed on every side, yet not crushed;
we are perplexed, but not in despair;
persecuted, but not forsaken;
struck down, but not destroyed—
always carrying about in the body
the dying of the Lord Jesus,
that the life of Jesus also may be manifested in our body.
For we who live are always delivered to death for Jesus' sake,
that the life of Jesus also may be manifested in our mortal flesh.
~ 2 Corinthians 4:8-11

Beloved, do not think it strange
concerning the fiery trial which is to try you,
as though some strange thing happened to you;
but rejoice to the extent that you partake of Christ's sufferings,
that when His glory is revealed,
you may also be glad with exceeding joy.
If you are reproached for the name of Christ, blessed are you,
for the Spirit of glory and of God rests upon you.
On their part He is blasphemed,
but on your part He is glorified ...
Yet if anyone suffers as a Christian, let him not be ashamed,
but let him glorify God in this matter.
~ 1 Peter 4:12-14, 16

Therefore I endure all things for the sake of the elect,
that they also may obtain the salvation
which is in Christ Jesus with eternal glory.
~ 2 Timothy 2:10

CHAPTER FIVE

GREATER IS HE THAT IS IN ME

The Peril of Battle Fatigue

I STOOD OUTSIDE the heavy wooden door waiting to enter the choir loft. The sanctuary was animated with sounds of happiness and greetings. Our church felt alive with the Spirit of God and His goodness.

Let's just say, the enemy wasn't too pleased.

My place in the choir line was behind an older member of the congregation who was unhappy with the recent church growth. As I was hugging a friend and laughing, Ruth suddenly turned around and snarled, "Shhhh! You're too loud!" Her softly wrinkled face contorted with pure hatred. I was stunned. The worship service hadn't begun. No one was being disrespectful or irreverent. We were merely celebrating the Lord. Ruth's venom gushed forth and sprayed me with the stench of evil. *Lord, help me. What do I do? Defend me, Lord.* Ruth wanted us removed from the pastorate. She was a bitter old soul.

I felt God's Spirit rising within me. In His mercy, God poured out His grace and gave me the courage to face my foe with His love. I extended my arms and gave Ruth a hug. I gently reminded her that the people were excited to worship God. Whoops. Big mistake. More poison sprayed my face, "Well, this is the Lord's house and everyone is too noisy. Especially you!"

The vicious words cut me deep. My eyes welled up with tears; my hands began to shake. *Father, help me.* With all the graciousness I could muster, I said, "Ruth, I'm so sorry you're offended."

"Well, you should know better!" she said.

Within moments, we filed into the choir loft. I smiled at the congregation, but on the inside I was a mess. *Father, help me forgive her. Please show me what to do.* During the greeting time, I again reached out to Ruth with God's love. This time the venom was gone. Her face softened. My God was with me through the attack. He heard me when I called.

From deep within me came these words: *For we do not wrestle against flesh and blood, but against principalities, against powers, against the rulers of the darkness of this age, against spiritual hosts of wickedness in the heavenly places* (Ephesians 6:12).

I found a strange comfort in these words, but the stubborn side of me argued with the Author. *I know, Lord. But she most definitely has skin on and chose to assault me.*

The Lord responded: *But the driving force behind her is your adversary. He is the one who wants to stop My work here. If he can get you and David distracted, he'll most certainly do it.*

Ruth chose to be a mouthpiece for him, but Satan is the liar and thief. Not Ruth. Don't fall into his trap.

The Lord had spoken truth to my wounded spirit. Or was it my wounded pride? Maybe. My spirit was hurting, for sure, but could pride be getting in the way too? It's so easy to let our ministry become *our* ministry. Could pride be a chink in the armor that gives Satan the go-ahead? Maybe. Probably.

This would be a good time for a thorough heart evaluation. Pride sneaks in like a slithering snake and hides in the grass. Its root cause is deception—deception of the heart, deception disguised in self-righteousness, deception of self-worth. *Our* ministry, *our* calling. Hmm. Something to think about.

These thoughts came out of nowhere. I wrote them in obedience to what God is speaking to me about this issue. Please apply them where necessary. Remember, there is, therefore, now no condemnation to those who love God and walk according to His Spirit (Romans 8:1, paraphrase). God wants to heal us and give us strength for the journey.

Let's continue.

As believers in the Lord Jesus Christ and ministers of His gospel, we must discern the spiritual struggle. Without this discernment, we do, in fact, become detoured from the task at hand. We spend valuable time and emotional energy wrestling with human adversaries (those who choose to be Satan's vessels of destruction) instead of prayerfully warring against the invisible powers of darkness that scheme and strategize behind the scenes. Ultimately, the goal of all spiritual warfare is to prevent the opening of doors for the advancement of the gospel.

Let that knowledge sink deep into your *knower*. A basic understanding and recognition of spiritual warfare is imperative when we find ourselves in the heat of battle. And you know what else? I'm learning that we can understand and recognize the spiritual warfare to the nth degree, but if we don't utilize the weapons, knowledge, and armor God provides, we will be swallowed up in defeat. Despair is always lurking outside the servant's door. Frustration and anger stand right behind despair. Knowledge means nothing unless we choose to engage in the battle at hand as a soldier of the Most High God.

Paul exhorts us to *put on the whole armor of God, that you may be able to stand against the wiles of the devil* (Ephesians 6:11). I love what the original Greek tells us here. The Greek word for "be able" is *dunamai* (doo-nam-ahee), meaning to "have power." The word combines power and willingness with inherent strength and action.[5]

Sometimes when I'm knee-deep in a struggle, my knees give way to the mire pulling me down. Anxiety is a personal demon I battle. But God's Word tells me that I'm not facing my adversary in my own strength. His Spirit within me gives the inherent strength and power to be victorious if I'm obedient to His instruction. And the same holds true for you. What is His instruction in this passage? Put on the whole armor of God.

Look with me as Paul explains the armor:

Therefore take up the whole armor of God, that you may be able [there's that word again] to withstand in the evil day, and having done all, to stand. Stand therefore, having girded your waist with truth, having put on the breastplate of righteousness, and having shod your feet with the preparation of the gospel of peace; above all, taking the shield of faith with which you will be able to quench all the fiery darts of the wicked one. And take the helmet of salvation, and the sword of the Spirit, which is the word of God; praying always with all prayer and supplication in the Spirit, being watchful to this end with all perseverance and supplication for all the saints. (Ephesians 6:13-18)

Did you catch the words *take up* and *put on?* Yes, we're clothed in robes of righteousness because of the blood of Jesus. That robe is a gift that comes with salvation. But in these verses, Paul uses action words in his instruction for victory—*take up, put on.* With intention, I might add.

If a soldier were to enter into battle without his weapons and body armor, we would consider him foolish. The same can be said for us. God has given us tools for victory. If we choose to dismiss His instruction, then we too may be deemed foolish. Spiritual warfare isn't some twilight-zone, freaky concept. According to the Word of God, it is reality for the believer. As surely as there is a God in heaven, there is a devil who roams this earth seeking whom he may devour. And he especially loves to go after God's faithful servants. Knowledge plus application equals victory.

In my research, I discovered some interesting facts about the pieces of armor Paul refers to. It helped me understand the depth of Paul's analogy. I mentioned the robe of righteousness that all believers in Jesus Christ have been given. The first piece of armor Paul mentions is the one that girds our waist with truth. In biblical times, all men wore robes. When they needed freedom to move about in demanding activities, the men tucked their long skirts into their belts—girded their loins. A girded robe signified readiness for action.[6] The New International Version phrases it this way: *with the belt of truth buckled around your waist* (Ephesians 6:14).

Not only is our robe of righteousness tucked up out of the way to prepare for action, but also the belt holding it in place is truth. That makes me think of our core muscles— our core being—the part of us that makes us strong. If our core is girded about with truth, then we know who we are and to whom we belong. We stand firm in the saving grace of the knowledge of Jesus. We know that if God is for us, no one can stand against us (Romans 8:31). We know that no weapon formed against us will prosper (Isaiah 54:17). And we know that the Lord will never leave us nor forsake us (Hebrews 13:5). Truth. Truth prepares us for battle, for we know in whom we have believed, and we know that we're not alone.

The next piece of armor Paul mentions is the breastplate of righteousness. Consider the time period in which Paul wrote, and picture Roman soldiers draped in battle armor. The breastplate was crucial to their survival. It protected their torso where all of the vital organs are found: heart, lungs, and liver, but especially the heart. Without the breastplate, the soldier faced imminent death, regardless of his skills and regardless of the remaining pieces of armor. He was vulnerable to the enemy's attack. But if he wore a breastplate, blows to the heart or other vital organs were deflected. The blows couldn't penetrate and destroy. The same is true for us in a spiritual sense.

Paul referred to our breastplate as the breastplate of righteousness. Oh my goodness. Satan will always try to strike us at the heart of our faith. You can be sure he knows our weaknesses and our vulnerabilities. But the Lord has not only given us a new heart; He also has covered our heart with the protection of His righteousness. *For He [God] made Him [Jesus] who knew no sin to be sin for us, that we might become the righteousness of God in Him* (2 Corinthians 5:21).

In my studies, I learned something that I can't wait to share with you: one of the many names of the Lord is *Jehovah-tsidkenu*, which means "The LORD Our Righteousness." I love that. God revealed this aspect of His character in Jeremiah 23:5-6:

> *"Behold, the days are coming," says the Lord, "when I will raise up to David a righteous Branch (Sprout), and He will reign as King and do wisely and will execute judgment and righteousness in the land. In His days Judah shall be saved, and Israel shall dwell safely; and this is His name by which He shall be called: The Lord Our Righteousness."* (AMP)

This is the promise of the new covenant for God's people. It's a covenant of grace and established by faith in the Lord Jesus Christ:

[God says,] "I will give you a new heart and put a new spirit within you; I will take the heart of stone out of your flesh and give you a heart of flesh. I will put My Spirit within you and cause you to walk in My statutes, and you will keep My judgments and do them. Then you shall dwell in the land that I gave to your fathers; you shall be My people, and I will be your God." (Ezekiel 36:26-28)

You shall be my people, and I will be your God. Let that promise sink in for a minute. *Jehovah-tsidkenu* is our righteousness, the protector of our hearts in the heat of battle. When we take up His breastplate of righteousness—when we say yes to Jesus—we can't be destroyed by the works of the enemy. We belong to our God.

The third piece of armor Paul mentions is shoes. What kind of shoes? Shoes that are *shod with the preparation of the gospel of peace.* If you're like me, this piece of armor has been the most difficult to understand in terms of significance. When I consider these shoes, my thoughts go to Isaiah 52:7 which reads, *How beautiful upon the mountains are the feet of him who brings good news, who proclaims peace, who brings glad tidings of good things, who proclaims salvation, who says to Zion, "Your God reigns!"* Paul even makes reference to this passage in Romans 10:14-15:

How then shall they call on Him in whom they have not believed? And how shall they believe in Him of whom they have not heard? And how shall they hear without a preacher? And how shall they preach unless they are sent? As it is written, "How beautiful are the feet of those who preach the gospel of peace."

This is pretty clear, but I still didn't understand how these shoes could be part of the armor of God, until—are you ready?

Again, picture the Roman soldier preparing for battle. The Roman soldier is Paul's point of reference for each article of armor. The soldier attached nails or spikes to the bottom of his sandals to assure a firm grip to the ground he covered in battle, especially rocky ground. (Think of modern cleats worn by athletes.) As an extension to these fortified sandals, the soldiers wore greaves—brass shields secured around their lower legs to defend them against danger or injury.

Together, the sandals and greaves provided foot protection much like a pair of boots. Think of it this way: if the feet or lower legs of the soldier became wounded, he couldn't stand to resist his enemy. Neither could he pursue his enemy. These pieces of armor ensured his ability to stand. Superior officers didn't wear these articles of armor; only the common soldiers wore them. Isn't that interesting?

Let's break it down. The foot armor Paul refers to provides protection in our travels, in our battles. Our foot armor ensures a firm foundation, a grip on the things of our faith so we won't falter under Satan's attacks. The firm foundation is the gospel of peace—the reconciliation between God and man. When we embrace who we are in Christ—when we walk in the knowledge that He is our God and that we belong to Him—our feet are prepared to take His message into all the world. This armor allows us to move forward against opposition because, once our *knower* is filled with the knowledge of what our salvation and relationship to Christ entails, we go forth on a firm foundation. The shoes equip us and prepare us to preach the Good News of peace with God—which makes an intimate relationship with Him possible—wherever He may send us.

And now the shield of faith. This may be my favorite piece of armor. Maybe that's because it's the easiest one for me to visualize. Remember the story I recounted at the beginning of this chapter? A vicious woman named Ruth verbally attacked me. She spewed poisonous words all over me as we waited outside the choir loft. The old Nan would have melted into a pool of hot tears and run to an empty classroom or ladies' room. I would have crumpled under the sting of her attack.

But God.

Don't you love that phrase?

But God has been teaching me to recognize the fiery darts of the enemy. How do you fend off fiery darts or flaming arrows? With a shield. A shield of faith. Does the shield of faith mysteriously appear in times of need? No. It's ours for the taking, but we must *raise* it high against the attack of the enemy—even when our flesh wants to convince us that we deserve a pity party. Just sayin'.

The Roman shield was a large rectangle (approximately three and a half feet tall and almost three feet wide), and slightly curved. The center of these shields featured a large metal knob called a boss. (Wait until I tell you the purpose of the boss!) Just the sheer size of the Roman shield offered great protection against the enemy. Its slightly curved design was ingenious because the attack could be deflected without transferring the full force to the soldier. The power of the attack was diffused into a more manageable force. The boss in the center allowed the soldiers to knock their opponent backward with a shove powerful enough to stun them. Brilliant. Our faith in God is that *boss* in the middle of our shield of faith.

What does a shield do? It guards, deflects, and incapacitates. The shield of faith is our first line of defense. When Satan hurls his fiery darts of fear, worry, and doubt in your direction, raise your shield of faith. Remind him that your God is able; He is faithful, merciful, and good. Remind him that you're a child of the Most High God, a daughter of the King. Use your boss and tell Satan you have been washed in the Blood of Jesus. Tell him that where the Blood has been applied, he has no authority and no dominion. Now that's what I'm talkin' about.

The helmet of salvation is the next piece of armor that will protect us against the enemy. The importance of wearing a helmet when engaged in potentially harmful activities can't be overemphasized. Think of the young bicyclist racing down a mountain trail. He hits a stone, which jerks the wheel, and the teenager somersaults over the handlebars onto a rocky ledge. His head rams a boulder, and he bounces to a stop. He lies still for a moment. Quiet. Shaken. Slowly, he sits up and lifts the helmet from his head. A bloody knee and scraped elbow testify to the unexpected acrobatics, but the biker is alive. His helmet protected him from sudden death.

That is the purpose of our helmet of salvation.

In the Roman army, the helmet protected the soldier's head from an enemy's deadly attacks. In our spiritual warfare, our helmet of salvation serves the same purpose. Satan can't access our spirit. Because of our salvation, we've been sealed by the Spirit of God, marking us as His own (2 Corinthians 1:21-22). But Satan most definitely has access to our mind and to our thoughts. That is the battle he consistently wages against us, and that is the battle he often wins. If we let him.

One verse I often recite is 2 Corinthians 10:5: *Casting down arguments and every high thing that exalts itself against the knowledge of God, bringing every thought into captivity to the obedience of Christ.* The New International Version reads this way: *We demolish arguments and every pretension that sets itself up against the knowledge of God, and we take captive every thought to make it obedient to Christ.* Notice the action words: *cast down, bring, demolish,* and *take captive.* Do you recognize a theme? Victory in spiritual warfare requires action on our part.

Is it hard to bring our thoughts captive to the Lord? Yes ma'am. It's tough. Especially for us girls. Our thoughts and imagination can run amuck really fast, right? We're vulnerable in this area, especially in relation to self-confidence, self-esteem, insecurity, and pride. You can be sure Satan knows our weak link. If he can penetrate our armor, he will. He loves fiery darts: *Zing! You're too fat. Zing! Did you hear what she said about you? Zing! Are you crazy? You* can't accomplish that. *God would never use you for something that special.* Our minds are his first line of attack.

What makes it even more difficult? We live in this world. We're influenced by its lies. As a woman, I know how much we compare ourselves to others. It's terrible, isn't it? We're *in* this world, but we are not to be *of* this world. Before His death, Jesus prayed for all of His disciples. He said, *"I do not pray that You should take them out of the world, but that You should keep them from the evil one. They are not of the world, just as I am not of the world"* (John 17:15-16). If Satan can get us to listen to his lies and surrender to the world's influence, he will defeat us. Simple as that. Our thoughts steer our feet, direct our decisions, and determine our focus. Satan knows that. Paul exhorts the Christians in Rome to *not be conformed to this world, but be transformed by the renewing of your mind, that you may prove what is that good and acceptable and perfect will of God* (Romans 12:2). The Greek word Paul uses for "renewing" is *anakainosis* (an-ak-ahee-no-sis), which means "a renovation, restoration, transformation, and a change of heart and life."[7] This transformation—this renewing—comes by surrendering to the Lordship of Christ, bringing our thoughts captive to Him in obedience to His Word. We are to develop the mind of Christ (Philippians 2:5). That can only come by writing His precious Word upon our hearts and giving it precedence over all the lies of Satan.

As Paul's life was coming to an end, he wrote the following in a letter to Timothy: *I have fought the good fight, I have finished the race, I have kept the faith. Finally, there is laid up for me the crown of righteousness, which the Lord, the righteous Judge, will give to me on that Day, and not to me only but also to all who have loved His appearing* (2 Timothy 4:7-8).

Take a moment to picture that in your mind. Paul understands that he'll trade in his soldier's helmet for a far more glorious, eternal crown of righteousness. This is a crown of victory for all of God's faithful servants.

That includes you.

The last piece of armor Paul mentions is the sword of the Spirit. The sword is the Word of God—the only offensive piece of our spiritual armor. All the other pieces defend us. Even if we're fully clothed with truth, righteousness, peace, faith, and salvation, without our sword we are basically heavily armored moving targets.[8] Our armor will most likely protect us against serious injury, but without the sword of the Spirit, we can't win. How can that be? Because it's the sword of the *Spirit*—the Word of God— full of power and authority. Its effectiveness has nothing to do with the intelligence or charm or manipulation of the child (soldier) of God. Nothing. It has everything to do with the Most High God.

Do you remember when Satan tempted Jesus in the wilderness? Jesus had been fasting and praying for forty days and nights. Satan knew He was hungry—he recognized Jesus' weak link. Satan tempted Jesus to turn the stones to bread; after all, He was the Son of God. How did Jesus respond? *"It is written, 'Man shall not live by bread alone, but by every word that proceeds from the mouth of God'"* (Matthew 4:4). Satan continued to tempt Jesus. He even tried to twist the meaning of the Scriptures in his quest to defeat Jesus. He told Jesus to throw Himself down from the pinnacle of the temple because God's Word promises the angels would protect Him. But Jesus recognized Satan's deception and responded, *"It is written again, 'You shall not tempt the Lord your God'"* (Matthew 4:7). Jesus defeated Satan by speaking the specific Scripture appropriate for the temptation through the power of the Spirit.

Let's look at this further. When Paul called this weapon of warfare "the sword of the Spirit, which is the Word of God," he used the Greek word *rhema* for word. *Rhema* refers to the spoken word whereas the Greek word *logos* refers to the written word. *Logos* is the message; *rhema* is the *communication* of the message. When the Word of God is functioning as the sword of the Spirit, the believer is speaking a specific portion of Scripture as a weapon targeted at their point of need.[9] This is done through the power of the Holy Spirit—*not* through the believer's own strength. The sword of the Spirit is a spiritual weapon. It's not a Bible gathering dust on our coffee table. Satan considers that display laughable. The power of this weapon comes when the Word of God is hidden in our hearts and spoken with authority through the Holy Spirit.

I didn't tell you the whole story of Ruth's verbal assault on me. When her attack of vicious words began, I told you that from deep within me came these words: *For we do not wrestle against flesh and blood, but against principalities, against powers, against the rulers of the darkness of this age, against spiritual hosts of wickedness in the heavenly places* (Ephesians 6:12). That is absolutely true. The Holy Spirit caused that Scripture to rise up within me because I needed it as a weapon to defeat Satan. So, in my spirit, I spoke that verse and ended with *get thee behind me, Satan, in the Name of Jesus*. This empowered me. It reminded me of Whose I am, but it also whipped around and thrust the power of God right into Satan's gut.

Can you see the picture of the boss on my shield? Can you see the swift action of the sword? Instead of melting into a hot mess, I stood strong in the power of God. I stood strong through the authority of His Word.

Paul's final instruction in this passage concerning spiritual warfare and the armor of God is to pray *always with all prayer and supplication in the Spirit, being watchful to this end with all perseverance* (Ephesians 6:18). *The Amplified Bible* makes it clearer: *Pray at all times (on every occasion, in every season) in the Spirit, with all [manner of] prayer and entreaty. To that end keep alert and watch with strong purpose and perseverance.* That last sentence is worth saying again: *To that end keep alert and watch with strong purpose* and *perseverance.* Watch. With Purpose. And Perseverance.

Have you ever thought about what happens when we pray? I mean, in the heavens—in the spiritual realm. Consider this: The Lord hears us the moment we pray and begins His response. If Satan's job is to steal, kill, and destroy (John 10:10), we can be sure he'll do what he can to prevent the blessing, the provision, or the answer from reaching us. But the Lord hears us as soon as we pray. Here's an illustration:

Our little country church was considered a community pillar, at least in days gone by. In its heyday, we were told, its walls were bursting with families. Church pews held many people hungrily searching for God. Excitement filled the halls; the glory of God beamed in the sanctuary. And then, as so often happens, a stillness settled on the congregation. Negativity permeated its heart. The church's outreach turned inward, extinguishing its light.

But God had other plans. He sent David and me to restore His joy to His church.

When we arrived, there was a strong sense of sadness and defeat. Week after week we worked diligently, but we made little headway. One Wednesday night after the church service, David and two other men became desperate for God. They began to pray earnestly—fervently—for God's favor. They boldly asked for revival.

The harder the men prayed, the stronger the spiritual opposition fought back. Let me say that again. The harder the men prayed, the stronger the spiritual opposition fought back. The men were tempted to give up, yet each of them understood they were engaged in a celestial battle. For weeks, the men sought God together, often into the wee hours of the morning. People sensed a stirring in the congregation, an awakening. The pews overflowed with church members who had long before left its chambers.

And then revival burst forth.

David baptized several people each Sunday. A drunken man showed up one Sunday. He said that God woke him in the night and that he knew he had to be saved. A prostitute appeared on another Sunday and walked away a new creation in Christ. Amazing! But I ask you: what would have happened if David and the men had stopped praying?

Goodness, do I have an answer for you. Are you ready? Let's look at Daniel, chapter ten. Daniel had been fasting and praying for twenty-one days, mourning over the plight of Israel. On the twenty-first day, an angel appeared to Daniel and said,

> *"Do not be afraid Daniel. Since the first day that you set your mind to gain understanding and to humble yourself before your God, your words were heard, and I have come in response to them. But the prince of the Persian kingdom resisted me twenty-one days. Then Michael, one of the chief princes, came to help me, because I was detained there with the king of Persia."*
> (Daniel 10:12-13 NIV)

Did you catch what the angel told Daniel in verse thirteen? He said that the prince of the Persian kingdom (a principality of darkness) resisted him for twenty-one days. Twenty-one days. The exact amount of time Daniel had been praying. The angel had been dispensed with an answer to Daniel's prayers the moment he began to pray, but it took him twenty-one days to reach Daniel because of the spiritual warfare. What if Daniel had stopped praying?

What if *you* stop praying about a particular situation?

What if I stop praying?

How often have we waited for God's intervention only to become distracted by the frustration of the seeming silence or to grow impatient with the slow progress? And in the distraction we cease to pray.

"Prayer is not so much a weapon, or even a part of the armor, as it is the means by which we engage in the battle itself and the purpose for which we're armed. To put on the armor of God is to prepare for battle. Prayer is the battle itself, with God's Word being our chief weapon employed against Satan during our struggle."[10] Oh my. Let me say that again, "To put on the armor of God is to *prepare* for battle. *Prayer is the battle itself.*" Not engaging in fistfights or shouting matches. Not engaging in backstabbing gossip or tongue-lashings. And certainly not surrendering to the enemy's tactics.

Pray, dear sister, pray. Fight the battle on your knees.

After all this talk of war, are you ready for a morsel of deliciousness? Jeremiah 33:1-3 says, *Moreover the word of the LORD came to Jeremiah a second time, while he was still shut up in the court of the prison, saying, "Thus says the LORD who made it, the LORD who formed it to establish it (the LORD is His name): 'Call to Me, and I will answer you, and show you great and mighty things, which you do not know'."*

How many times have you read this and thought, "Wow! Good things are coming my way"? I know I've thought that. We should expect the Lord to hear us when we pray. Absolutely. But the great and mighty things aren't things at all. The Hebrew word for "mighty" is *batsar*, which means "inaccessible." When we call out to God—I mean really call out from our gut with desperation and passion —He'll show us "revelational insight, revealing things that otherwise would be inaccessible."[11]

This insight from God will lead us to victory in the spiritual warfare. It will open our eyes to see the heart of the person or persons who hurt us and slander our good names. It will open our eyes to see the eternal purposes of God, especially in our personal pain.

That is amazing.

Notice that Jeremiah was in prison when the Lord spoke these words to him. Prison. God's servant was in prison, yet he wasn't alone. Not only that, but God opened Jeremiah's eyes to see.

Delicious.

Promises for the Peril of Battle Fatigue

When you go out to battle against your enemies,
and see horses and chariots and people more numerous than you,
do not be afraid of them; for the LORD your God is with you,
who brought you up from the land of Egypt.
So it shall be, when you are on the verge of battle,
that the priest shall approach and speak to the people.
And he shall say to them, "Hear, O Israel;
Today you are on the verge of battle with your enemies.
Do not let your heart faint, do not be afraid,
and do not tremble or be terrified because of them;
for the LORD your God is He who goes with you,
to fight for you against your enemies, to save you."
~ Deuteronomy 20:1-4

But the Lord stood with me and strengthened me,
so that the message might be preached fully through me,
and that all the Gentiles might hear.
Also I was delivered out of the mouth of the lion.
And the Lord will deliver me from every evil work
and preserve me for His heavenly kingdom.
To Him be glory forever and ever. Amen!
~ 2 Timothy 4:17-18

For You have armed me with strength for the battle;
You have subdued under me those who rose against me.
~ 2 Samuel 22:40

CHAPTER SIX

JOY IN THE WILDERNESS

The Peril of Despair

MY SISTER, THIS chapter is pivotal to your healing. May I pray for you before we begin?

> *Father God, Your love for us astounds me. Your love is persistent, merciful, full of grace and oh so palpable. Open our eyes to see You in our midst. Open our hearts to find You in our pain and struggles. You, Lord, are our great reward. No other one compares with You. I lift up my sister to You and ask that You grant her understanding of Your Presence, of how You are drawn to our brokenness. What a comfort it is to know You are with us always and that You are ever ready to lift us above the turbulence of the storm. You are our strength. You are our God. And You are our joy. We love You, Lord.*

My mom died of breast cancer at the age of forty-six. I was twenty. I was also a new Christian, having met Jesus a year before her illness. I stormed the gates of heaven for my mom's healing, and yet she died. I was devastated. My newfound faith was shaken. My bustling young life spiraled downward into a pit of numbness and dark silence.

A close friend gave me the book, *Hinds' Feet on High Places* by Hannah Hurnard. This powerful book is an allegory of our Christian journey. It's the story of a young pilgrim, Much-Afraid, who is traveling with her two companions, Sorrow and Suffering. They're journeying to the High Places to meet the Chief Shepherd. Much-Afraid is the one who taught me to find joy in my wilderness places. The following is an excerpt from this exceptional book:

Last of all he took her up the stairway to the highest floor. There they found a room with a furnace in which gold was being smelted and refined of all its dross. Also in the furnace were rough pieces of stone and rock containing crystals. These were put in the great heat of the oven and left for a time. On being taken out, behold, they were glorious jewels, flashing as though they had received the fire into their very hearts. As Much-Afraid stood beside the Shepherd, looking shrinkingly into the fire, he said the loveliest thing of all.

"O thou afflicted, tossed with tempest, and not comforted, behold, I will lay thy stones with fair colors,

and lay thy foundations with sapphires. And I will make thy windows of agates, and thy gates of carbuncles, and all thy borders of pleasant stones" (Isaiah 54:11). Then he added, "My rarest and choicest jewels and my finest gold are those who have been refined in the furnace of Egypt," and he sang one verse of a little song:

> "I'll turn my hands upon thy heart,
>   And purge away thy dross,
>   I will refine thee in my fire,
>   Remake thee at my cross."

They stayed at the huts in the desert for several days, and Much-Afraid learned many things which she had never heard before.

One thing, however, made a special impression upon her. In all that great desert, there was not a single green thing growing, neither tree nor flower nor plant save here and there a patch of straggly grey cacti.

On the last morning she was walking near the tents and huts of the desert dwellers, when in a lonely corner behind a wall she came upon a little golden-yellow flower, growing all alone. An old pipe was connected with a water tank. In the pipe was one tiny hole through which came an occasional drop of water. Where the drops fell one by one, there grew the little golden flower, though where the seed had come from, Much-Afraid could not imagine, for there were no birds anywhere and no other growing things.

She stopped over the lonely, lovely little golden face, lifted up so hopefully and so bravely to the feeble drip, and cried out softly, "What is your name, little flower, for I never saw one like you before?"

The tiny plant answered at once in a tone as golden as itself, "Behold me! My name is Acceptance-with-Joy."

Much-Afraid thought of the things which she had seen in the pyramid: the threshing-floor and the whirring wheel and the fiery furnace. Somehow the answer of the little golden flower which grew all alone in the waters of the desert stole into her heart and echoed there faintly but sweetly, filling her with comfort. She said to herself, "He has brought me here when I did not want to come for his own purpose. I, too, will look up into his face and say, 'Behold me! I am thy little handmaiden Acceptance-with-Joy'." Then she stooped down and picked up a pebble which was lying in the sand beside the flower and put it in the purse with the first altar stone.[12]

I know, right? I'll wait here while you grab a tissue. This is powerful stuff, isn't it? Well, get ready. I'm going to blow your socks off. Remember, I first read this book shortly after my mom died. I was a devastated young woman trying desperately to hold on to the hand of Jesus.

I read through that section of *Hinds' Feet on High Places* and then set the book down on my bed. I needed to walk. I needed to think. I needed to pray. I grabbed a light jacket and walked out into our backyard. The days had been crisp because an early fall settled into the Charlotte area. Dad was a gardener, filling his days with tilling the ground God had given him. Our backyard brimmed with plants and trees. Daddy especially enjoyed azaleas. If you've ever traveled south, you're familiar with the glorious azaleas of spring. Their delightful shades of pink, purple, fuchsia, and red stir up the joys of new beginnings after long, cold winters.

Like I said, they bloom in the spring.

Momma died on September 2, 1975.

I stood in the backyard, tears streaming, my heart breaking. I implored the Lord to help me come to terms with Momma's death. I begged Him to help me find His joy in this wilderness—this desert place.

I wiped my tears with the sleeve of my jacket. Out of the corner of my eye, I saw a pop of fuchsia in the fall foliage. *What is that?* I walked over to a cluster of azaleas at the base of an oak tree. There, surrounded by leaves beginning their fall sabbatical, was one, solitary bloom. An azalea bloom. In September. In Charlotte, NC. Oh my goodness!

"Lord, You heard me!" I shouted to the heavens. "You've given me my joy in the wilderness, my little Acceptance-with-Joy. Thank You, Lord. Thank You for loving me so much. Help me to walk in Your joy."

Can you imagine? I mean, really. God, the Creator of the Universe, did that for me. Well, guess what? It gets better. Are you ready? Fast-forward twenty-eight years.

Daddy was beginning to let go of this world. Leukemia ravaged his body, but Jesus strengthened his soul. He reached his hands toward heaven and mumbled something indiscernible. My stepmom and I stood at his bedside, keeping him comfortable, waiting for the inevitable. "Go to the Light, Daddy. We'll be okay. Please, go to the Light." And he did.

My heart was broken. I wandered from his bedroom and stared numbly out the window. I thanked God for my dad. I asked the Lord to hold me, to comfort me with His love. And then I asked Him for something extraordinary. I asked Him for joy in the wilderness, my very own Acceptance-with-Joy.

I looked out of the bay window toward the sidewalk. I could see something fuchsia among the fall foliage. I stepped outside and stood in wide-eyed amazement. This time it was the end of October in Charlotte, NC. Yes, I said the end of October. There among the leaves beginning their fall sabbatical was a solitary bloom. An azalea bloom. In Charlotte. In October. Imagine! God had heard my cry once again.

I raised my face toward heaven, and with tears coursing down my cheeks, gave praise to my Jesus. He had kissed me with His grace. I felt the arms of everlasting Love enfold me. God's peace flooded my heart and filled in the broken places with the joy of His Presence.

Joy in the wilderness. Acceptance-with-Joy.

Am I someone special? No. God is no respecter of persons. Each of us is His special treasure. He pursues us with His love. He delights in revealing His goodness to His children. So I'm no more special than you are, but I set my heart, my mind, my soul, and my strength to find joy in my wilderness. I opened my eyes to see the Spirit of God with me, to find acceptance of His will with joy. And I'm learning—*He* is our joy, our great reward.

The word of the LORD came to Abram in a vision, saying, "Do not be afraid, Abram. I am your shield, your exceedingly great reward" (Genesis 15:1). This profound statement came shortly before the Lord made the famous covenant with Abram—the covenant that we are now partakers of through the blood of Jesus (Genesis 17:7; Galatians 3:13-20). God said, *"I am Almighty God; walk before Me and be blameless. And I will make My covenant between Me and you, and will multiply you exceedingly." Then Abram fell on his face, and God talked with him, saying: ... "No longer shall your name be called Abram, but your name shall be Abraham"* (Genesis 17:1-3, 5).

Notice Abram's name changed from Abram to Abraham after the covenant. Why is this significant? Because the letter *h*, which is part of Abram's new name, is also part of God's name—*Yahweh*. In the Hebrew tradition, people were named because of something that marked them, whether physical features, character traits, or accomplishments, either expected or achieved. Someone's name represented the very essence of who they were. When the Lord gave Abram a new name as a reflection of the covenant between them, I believe the meaning of this action is profound. God gave a part of Himself to Abram. He marked Abraham as His own. God took a portion of Himself, of His name *Yahweh*—I AM WHO I AM—and gave it to Abram. I AM anything and everything you need Me to be. An exchange occurred in the covenant between Abram and the Lord, just as an exchange occurs between us and the Lord when we enter into this covenant through His Son Jesus. We exchange our weakness for His strength, our despair for His peace. We exchange our sorrow for His joy, and He fills us with a portion of Himself. He becomes our God and we become His people. We discover our great reward: the Lord God Himself.

I stand amazed at the thought of how much the Lord wants us to know Him. I mean really know Him, not just about Him. From beginning to end, the salvation story is a beautiful love story between God, the Creator of the Universe, and His children. When we awaken our hearts to receive this love fully, we find our reward. We discover that joy is no longer contingent on circumstances. It is based completely on understanding to whom we belong. In Psalm 43, David asks God to help him during a time of trouble. In verse four he says, *"Then I will go to the altar of God, to God my exceeding joy; and on the harp I will praise You, O God, my God."* (Please don't miss the word *go*. God didn't just pop up. David sought Him.)

I used to have God in a box. Oh, it was a beautiful box, for sure, but a box nevertheless. This box was gilded with the finest gold, lined with the purest silver, and embellished with rubies, emeralds, sapphires, and diamonds. Oh yes. It was a fine box. Only the best for the Lord. But here's the problem. God is too grand to contain. We're limited in our ability to comprehend Him; therefore, we limit God to the perimeters of our understanding. Our limitations place Him in the proverbial box. But if we are to understand how the Lord is to be our great reward, our exceeding joy, then we must delve into a greater understanding of Who He is. We have to take Him out of the box. Are you ready?

Let's go back to I AM WHO I AM, which is the basic translation of *Yahweh* (or *YHWH*). When God selected Moses to deliver His people from slavery in Egypt, Moses wasn't a happy camper. He dared to challenge the Lord: *"Indeed, when I come to the children of Israel and say to them, 'The God of your fathers has sent me to you,' and they say to me, 'What is His name?' what shall I say to them?"* (Exodus 3:13).

The Lord responded, *"I AM WHO I AM."* And He said, *"Thus you shall say to the children of Israel, 'I AM has sent me to you'"* (Exodus 3:14). The issue isn't who Moses is, but WHO is with him.

The issue isn't who we are, but WHO is with us.

I AM is with us. Our great reward. Our exceeding joy.

I like to think of the name, I AM WHO I AM, in terms of an umbrella. I AM WHO I AM forms the arc along the top of the umbrella. Beneath the arc are many names, each representing different attributes and character traits of the Lord. There are representative names such as *Jehovah-jireh*, the Lord who provides; *Jehovah-rapha*, the Lord who heals. We've already looked at *Jehovah-tsidkenu*, the Lord my righteousness. One of my favorite names of God is *El Roi*, the God Who Sees Me. He identifies Himself by this name in the story of Hagar.

God promised Abram that he would be the father of many nations. For almost ten years, Abram had waited for the promised son who would be the beginning of his great legacy. His wife, Sarai, was seventy-five years old. She had exhausted her faith. She and Abram were getting older by the minute, so she took matters into her own hands. Sarai gave her maidservant, Hagar, to Abram for the purpose of conceiving a child. *So he [Abram] went in to Hagar, and she conceived. And when she saw that she had conceived, her mistress became despised in her eyes* (Genesis 16:4). Sarai became very upset. She accused Abram of being the source of her problems. He told her that Hagar, as her maidservant, was her business, and Sarai could deal with her as she pleased. Sarai dealt so harshly with Hagar that Hagar fled into the wilderness:

> *Now the Angel of the LORD found her by a spring of water in the wilderness, by the spring on the way to Shur. And He said, "Hagar, Sarai's maid, where have you come from, and where are you going?" She said, "I am fleeing from the presence of my mistress Sarai." The Angel of the LORD said to her, "Return to your mistress, and submit yourself under her hand." Then the Angel of the LORD said to her, "I will multiply your descendants exceedingly, so that they shall not be counted for multitude."* (Genesis 16:7-10)

In verse thirteen, we find the first mention of God's name, *El Roi: Then she [Hagar] called the name of the LORD who spoke to her, [El Roi] "You are a God who sees"; for she said, "Have I also here seen Him who sees me?"*

Fifteen years later, Isaac was born to Abraham, age 100, and Sarah, age 90. (God had changed their names in Genesis 17 as a sign of the new covenant.) Once again, Hagar encountered Sarah's animosity. *Therefore she [Sarah] said to Abraham, "Cast out this bondwoman and her son; for the son of this bondwoman shall not be heir with my son, namely with Isaac"* (Genesis 21:10). Abraham rose early the next morning and gave Hagar bread, water, and her son, Ishmael, and sent them into the wilderness. It wasn't long before their provisions were used up. Hagar then placed her son under a bush:

> *Then she went and sat down across from him at a distance of about a bowshot; for she said to herself, "Let me not see the death of the boy." So she sat opposite him, and lifted her voice and wept. And God heard the voice of the lad. Then the angel of God called to Hagar out of heaven, and said to her, "What ails you, Hagar? Fear not, for God has heard the voice of the lad where he is."* (Genesis 21:16-17)

God opened her eyes and she saw a well of water—life-sustaining water. The Bible tells us that Ishmael and Hagar dwelt there in the wilderness as he grew. *El Roi* had seen the injustice done to them. He saw their pain. He heard their cries. And He met their needs. *El Roi*—the God Who Sees Me and knows all about it.

This leads me to one of my favorite verses, 2 Chronicles 16:9: *For the eyes of the LORD run to and fro throughout the* whole earth, to show Himself strong on behalf of those whose heart is loyal to Him. The *Amplified Bible* reads this way: *The eyes of the LORD search the whole earth in order to strengthen those whose hearts are fully committed to Him.* Isn't that beautiful? What a thought! The One who holds the seas in the hollow of His hands, the One who walks on the wings of the wind and the clouds are but the dust of His feet—the Lord your God is *El Roi*, the God who sees your struggle and knows all about it. He is our exceedingly great reward. He is our exceeding joy in the wilderness.

Would you like another example?

Elijah was a mighty prophet and servant of God. I believe he was a humble man doing his best to walk in obedience to the Lord, just like you and your husband. Elijah certainly had God's favor upon him. But he encountered a woman named Jezebel.

Jezebel, King Ahab's wife, spent her days killing the prophets of God. (Remember that name. You've probably met her too.) Jezebel had her eye on Elijah and set in motion a plan to kill him.

> Then Jezebel sent a messenger to Elijah, saying, "So let the gods do to me, and more also, if I do not make your life as the life of one of them [these men were dead] by tomorrow about this time." And when he [Elijah] saw that, he arose and ran for his life, and went to Beersheba, which belongs to Judah, and left his servant there.
> (1 Kings 19:2-3)

Elijah was running for his life. He had challenged and defeated 450 prophets of Baal (see 1 Kings 18:20-40), he had revealed the glory and power of the Lord in the challenge, and he clearly walked in the favor of God, *yet* he was now running for his life. My goodness! I can certainly relate. Can you? Let's see what happens next.

But he [Elijah] himself went a day's journey into the wilderness, and came and sat down under a broom tree. And he prayed that he might die, and said, "It is enough! Now, LORD, take my life, for I am no better than my fathers!" (1 Kings 18:3-4). Elijah was so despondent, so tired and worn, that he wanted to die. This ministry/servant gig had become a bit much. I'm encouraged to know that even our great heroes of faith wanted to give up sometimes. But, get ready, I'm about to warm your heart.

Let's look at verses 5-8:

Then as he lay and slept under a broom tree, suddenly an angel touched him, and said to him, "Arise and eat." Then he looked, and there by his head was a cake baked on coals and a jar of water. So he ate and drank, and lay down again. And the angel of the LORD came back the second time, and touched him, and said, "Arise and eat, because the journey is too great for you." So he arose, and ate and drank, and he went in the strength of that food forty days and forty nights as far as Horeb [Mt. Sinai], the mountain of God.

Dear one, don't miss how God responded to His faithful servant. The Angel of the Lord came to feed him and minister to his weary soul. The tenderness of God met the needs of His child and gave him the strength he needed for the journey.

God was Elijah's exceeding joy in the wilderness.

He was our joy in the wilderness when David and I met Jezebel.

In the spring of that year, a mockery of God's holiness entered our sanctuary. Its vessel was a woman who enjoyed control. A Jezebel. Leaders cowered in her presence and catered to her demands. She had held the church back for many years—long before we got there—all the while projecting a false humility, a false righteousness. She stood ready to take on David, the man of God, and to stop the fresh movement of the Holy Spirit. Why? He refused to be a yes-man to her. He refused to bow to her. David preaches the Word of God with power and authority. He doesn't play the religion game, and he tries to walk in obedience to the Lord.

The more the Spirit of God worked in our midst restoring lives and setting the captives free, the more agitated Jezebel became. At first, she insulted David in private conversations or manipulated and controlled people to get her own way when it came time for church-wide decisions. If someone expressed support for David or appreciation for all he was accomplishing in this once stale church, this woman scorned them and publically belittled them. Over time, she became more brazen, bringing her rebellion into the sanctuary.

Jezebel mocked my husband as he preached God's Word. She twisted her face in evil smirks when he looked in her direction, squinting her eyes at him. Her lips moved as though she were cursing him under her breath. She became so bold in her self-righteousness that on one occasion she elbowed one of her cohorts sitting next to her, making fun of someone as they approached the altar in tears. I kid you not. Why didn't someone do something about this? Because she was a deacon's wife and because everyone was afraid of her wrath.

Everyone, that is, but David.

My man didn't give in to her. He preached the Word with conviction; he held up the shield of faith, and he looked to his Redeemer for guidance. David's flesh was in agony, but his spirit remained strong. I thought I would collapse under the pressure, but, in His infinite mercy, God poured out His grace and gave us both the strength to endure.

David didn't compromise the Word of God. He openly addressed the rebellion from the pulpit, repeatedly offering opportunity for repentance. He cried over this woman's soul, knowing full well that without repentance she would remain separated from God. But she wouldn't budge. Her self-righteousness and pride blinded her to the need for God's saving grace.

After weeks of this, Jezebel's rebellion was growing like a cancer in the midst of the congregation. The church members weren't entering into her rebellion, but, because of the tension in the sanctuary, worship was null and void. It was horrible. It became impossible to find rest, hope, peace—whatever was needed—in these horrid circumstances. The deacons weren't willing to confront Jezebel and her behavior. David knew that as long as he remained the pastor, the battle would continue. After much prayer, we knew it was time to leave.

I am reminded of Job's powerful statement: *"I know that my Redeemer lives, and that in the end He will stand upon the earth. And after my skin has been destroyed, yet in my flesh I will see God; I myself will see Him with my own eyes—I, and not another. How my heart yearns within me!"* (Job 19:25-27 NIV). Job had his eyes on the prize, on his exceedingly great reward. He knew that he was chosen of God. He knew that everything about this earth is temporal—a mere snap of the fingers. In essence, Job said, "No matter what happens in my life, I will place my hope and my trust in my Redeemer. Why? I know my God and my God knows me." Job knew that after he suffered a little while, he would behold the Lord, face-to-face, in all of His glory.

David and I can say the same.

So can you.

Like Elijah, the tenderness of God came to us and met the needs of His children. In our brokenness, people came to us in love. They wrapped their arms around us and prayed. They thanked us for the goodness of God we had poured into their lives. God fed us with His grace, binding our wounds, and giving us the strength needed for the journey.

Once again, the Lord reminded us of His promise in 2 Chronicles 16:9: *For the eyes of the Lord run to and fro throughout the whole earth, to show Himself strong on behalf of those whose heart is loyal to Him.* Focus on—

ponder—those words for a minute. Let them sink into your *knower* because they're quite remarkable. The God of the Universe responds to our pain like a magnet to a piece of steel. It's innate—it can't be separated from His character. Oh my goodness! I find such comfort in this. He's always searching for the moments we need His strength and reassurance. Ask the Lord to open the eyes of your heart to see this image—the image of our magnificent God riding across the heavens to get to us in our time of need.

Now that's some good stuff.

If God is our exceedingly great reward and joy, then finding joy in the wilderness actually means finding God in our darkest moments. Do you see the connection? It took me many years to understand this seemingly simple concept, yet I believe that's because this truth is found in the hidden mysteries of Christ—those secret treasures that only God's children are allowed to find (Isaiah 45:3).

It began one day when I was studying the Word. One of my favorite passages of Scripture is John 15:4. Jesus said, *"Abide in Me, and I in you. As the branch cannot bear fruit of itself, unless it abides in the vine, neither can you, unless you abide in Me."* For years, I was drawn to this verse, but there was something that I always questioned. Finally, I boldly asked for understanding. "Lord, I understand how You abide in me. That's easy. I know Your Holy Spirit has been within me since the day Jesus became my Savior, but how do I dwell in You? I don't understand."

That's when He opened my eyes. When we walk closely—intimately—with the Lord, we're surrounded by

His Presence, immersed in His Spirit. How else could He hold our hand (Isaiah 41:13)? How else could He hedge us behind and before (Psalm 139:5)? What a comforting thought. Imagine: when we look ahead, He is there. He goes before us on this journey. If we look behind us, He is there also, supporting us, protecting us like a rearguard. He is with us, holding our hand. We're not alone. The more I prayed and sought the Lord about this, the more He opened my eyes.

As I tried to understand His Presence surrounding me always, I asked Him how I could dwell in darkness if He is light. He led me to 2 Chronicles 6:1-2: *Then Solomon spoke: "The LORD has said that He would dwell in a dark cloud."* Huh? The Lord is in a dark cloud? How is that possible? The following is an excerpt from my journal on the day the Lord gave me understanding:

The wind was kicking up, swirling fallen leaves into tiny whirlwinds. A thunderhead was forming on the horizon. As the massive clouds streamed overhead, the sun became obscured. I rocked on my porch and watched darkness settle on the mountainside.

I looked up at the afternoon sky, thick with dark storm clouds. I pondered what Solomon had said. I was looking for answers. I was looking for hope. Life had been so difficult lately. I knew we hadn't been forsaken by the Lord, but I couldn't put the pieces together. God is light and love and all things wonderful, so if I belonged to Him, how could life be filled with such darkness? There had to be an answer.

The sun peaked out from behind the darkest cloud in the sky. It was only for a moment, but it was a God-moment. As the sun revealed its crown of brilliant light, the cloud grew darker. Why? Could it be the darkness of the cloud is actually a shadow cast by the glorious light of the sun? That makes sense, doesn't it? Without the presence of the sun, I don't believe the cloud would be dark. The darkness is a shadow.

Solomon said the Lord told him He would dwell in a dark cloud. Exodus 20:21 reads, *The people remained at a distance, while Moses approached the thick darkness where God was* (NIV). I'm beginning to realize that throughout the Old Testament God shrouded His glory with a cloud. I had always pictured this cloud as being bright. But if God is *in* the cloud, the cloud itself would become dark because God's light would cast a shadow.

When I understand that God is with me and yet find myself in a dark place, could the darkness actually be *because* He is with me? Could it be that the brilliant Light of His Presence overshadows the evil invading my life? If so, then the reality of my darkness becomes the reality of His Presence.

Let that sink in: the reality of my darkness is the reality of His Presence.

I'm learning to press in. I'm learning to stop what I'm doing and run to Him, falling at His feet and clinging to the hem of His garment. Dishes can wait. Laundry will be there tomorrow. The Lord our God yearns to comfort us when we hurt, to smother us with His love. Can it really be that simple? Yes!

But we have to choose Him over the circumstances we're drowning in. As I learn more and more about His Presence (remember He said, "Abide *in* Me"), the eyes of my heart are grasping the knowledge that He really is with me. Always. God, the Creator of the Universe, is with me even now. And He's with you even now. We don't have to conjure up His Presence. We don't need to spend thirty minutes in prayer followed by reading one chapter in the Old Testament, one chapter in the New Testament, and five psalms. Oh. I forgot—add a chapter or two of Proverbs while you're at it. No! (Did I just shout? Yep.) The Lord desires us, not our religiosity. He's already with us. We need only open our eyes to see and then run to Him as fast as our little legs will carry us. Pour out your heart before Him. Devour His Word— absolutely—but not out of some religious requirement. Devour it because you're desperate to find the Lord in your midst.

In Acts 17:27-28, Paul explains that the Lord made all of mankind *so that they should seek the Lord, in the hope that they might grope for Him and find Him though*

He is not far from each one of us; for in Him we live and move and have our being. That's amazing, isn't it? Seeking. Groping. Finding. Because of the pain I've endured as a pastor's wife, my spirit stirs when I think about these words: we were created so that we would seek the Lord, and the Father's heart hoped that, in our darkness, we might grope for Him and find Him. The Lord knew that life on this earth wouldn't be easy for His children because it's sin-filled. It's Satan's domain. And yet He made a way for us to endure until we cross that golden shore. We endure through Him and in Him, *for in Him we live and move and have our being.* In Him.

King David wrote, *in Your presence is fullness of joy* (Psalm 16:11). Take a moment and let that image fill your mind: in His Presence, in Him, surrounded and immersed in His love, we find fullness of joy, for He is our joy. *The Pulpit Commentary* describes this fullness of joy as "satiety of joy—enough, and more than enough, to satisfy the extremest cravings of the human heart."[13] My goodness, what a powerful description: He satisfies the extreme cravings of our heart. Not with things. Not with people or places. He satisfies us with Himself. When we seek Him—when we grope for Him in our darkness—we will find Him. And when we find Him, we will find our joy in the wilderness.

In Frances J. Roberts' *Come Away My Beloved*, the Spirit of God speaks the following words. Awaken your heart to receive from the Lord.

A Song at Midnight

Behold, I am near at hand to bless you,
and I will surely give to you out of the abundance of heaven.
For My heart is open to your cry; yes,
when you cry to Me in the night seasons,
I am alert to your call, and when you search after Me,
the darkness will not hide My face;
it will be as the stars which shine more brightly in
the deep of the night.
Even so it shall be. In the night of spiritual battle,
there I shall give you fresh revelations of Myself,
and you shall see Me more clearly than you could
in the sunlight of ease and pleasure.
Man by nature chooses the day and shuns the night;
but I say to you,
I shall make your midnight a time of great rejoicing,
and I will fill the dark hour with songs of praise.
Yes, with David, you shall rise at midnight to sing.
It has been written, 'Joy comes in the morning,'
but I will make your song break out in the night.
For he who lifts the shout of faith and praise *in the night,*
to him there *shall* be joy in the morning.[14]

He'll make your midnight a time of great rejoicing,
and fill the dark hour with songs of praise. My sister, the

reality of your darkness is the reality of His Presence—
your joy in the wilderness. *Selah.*

Promises for the Peril of Despair

For in the time of trouble
He shall hide me in His pavilion;
In the secret place of His tabernacle
He shall hide me;
He shall set me high upon a rock.
And now my head shall be lifted up
above my enemies all around me;
Therefore I will offer sacrifices of joy in His tabernacle;
I will sing, yes, I will sing praises to the LORD.
Hear, O LORD, when I cry with my voice!
Have mercy also upon me, and answer me.
~ Psalm 27:5-7

Therefore we also, since we are surrounded
by so great a cloud of witnesses,
let us lay aside every weight,
and the sin which so easily ensnares us,
and let us run with endurance
the race that is set before us,
looking unto Jesus,
the author and finisher of our faith,
who for the joy that was set before Him
endured the cross, despising the shame,

and has sat down at the right hand of the throne of God.
For consider Him who endured such hostility
from sinners against Himself,
lest you become weary and discouraged in your souls.
~ Hebrews 12:1-3

In this you greatly rejoice,
though now for a little while, if need be,
you have been grieved by various trials,
that the genuineness of your faith,
being much more precious than gold that perishes,
though it is tested by fire,
may be found to praise, honor and glory
at the revelation of Jesus Christ,
whom having not seen you love.
Though now you do not see Him, yet believing,
you rejoice with joy inexpressible
and full of glory, receiving the end of your faith—
the salvation of your souls.
~ 1 Peter 1:6-9

CHAPTER SEVEN

COME TO ME

The Peril of Thirst

Now we begin walking (inching?) toward wholeness once again. The journey has been difficult thus far. I know. It's tough for me to relive these wounds too. But, praise God, when we learn to find Him in our pain, the healing becomes even sweeter.

Another entry from my journal illustrates my early lessons in understanding these truths. It began when I opened my ears to hear His sweet whisper: "Come to Me."

My heart had become hardened like a slab of granite. There were no more tears to wash away the debris left behind from months of gut-wrenching angst. My spirit lay dormant and neglected. I could feel the rushing of the Living Water deep in my soul, but I denied its access to my wounded spirit. The Holy Spirit pressed hard against my hardened heart, yearning to flood my soul with the fullness of God, but I resisted. I resisted and my heart became harder—fallow, Hosea might say. In fact, that is exactly what he said, *Sow for yourselves righteousness; reap the fruit of unfailing love, and break up your unplowed ground; for it is time to seek the LORD, until He comes and showers righteousness on you.* (Hosea 10:12 NIV)

Unplowed ground. Fallow. Hard as a brickbat.

"Break up your unplowed ground," Hosea declared, *"for it is time to seek the Lord."* A hardened heart that belongs to God will eventually crumble under the weight of its rebellion; it will break under the hand of a persistent God. Imagine a gardener wielding a hoe, striking the parched earth over and over—not to destroy her garden but to prepare the fallow ground to receive and absorb the life-giving water.

I'm learning to embrace my brokenness. I realize it has created fertile soil on which to receive the Word of God. The Gardener's calloused hand has broken through the hardness and gently pushed the soil aside to make the perfect place for His seed of righteousness. He waters it liberally with His Living Water causing the seed to take root, its tendrils branching out into the hidden crevices of my heart. His seed of righteousness has grown strong and bears the fruit of unfailing love, God's mercy. Each day I am wrapped in His precious gift, blanketed by His grace and love.

The Lord wants us to understand that it is He, and He alone, who can turn our bitterness into the fruit of unfailing love—that our bitter waters can taste beautifully sweet because of Him. Here's the lesson:

So Moses brought Israel from the Red Sea; then they went out into the Wilderness of Shur. And they went three days in the wilderness and found no water. Now when they came to Marah, they could not drink the waters of Marah, for they were bitter. Therefore the name of it was called Marah [bitter]. And the people complained against Moses, saying, "What shall we drink?"
(Exodus 15:22-24)

Let's put this in context. The Israelites had been delivered from Egypt about a month and a half earlier. They miraculously passed through the Red Sea and were traveling through the Wilderness of Shur. For three days, they traveled with no water. Hot, weary, overwhelmingly thirsty—these words don't begin to describe their need. Can you imagine traveling in the desert for three days with no water? Finally, they came upon a pool, but it was bitter—so bitter they couldn't drink it. Oh my goodness! Would the Lord lead them to bitter water? Would the God who had parted the Red Sea for His children lead them to this dreadful place? Why would He do that? After all the miracles of their deliverance from Egypt, why would

God lead His children to a place of bitter water? Because He had a huge lesson for them. As is true for us, God's intention was to teach them an eternal purpose behind their suffering. Let's dig deep to find the nugget of gold.

So he [Moses] cried out to the LORD, and the LORD showed him a tree. When he cast it into the waters, the waters were made sweet (Exodus 15:25). The Lord showed Moses a tree and told him to throw the tree into the bitter water. What was the result? The water was made sweet. How? How could this possibly have any significance for them, and especially for us? Read 1 Peter 2:24 for the answer: *[Jesus] bore our sins in His own body on the tree, that we, having died to sins, might live for righteousness—by whose stripes you were healed.* Do you see the correlation? A tree, ordained by God, was thrown into the putrid waters and soaked up the bitterness, making it sweet. A tree, ordained by God, held our precious Savior. God plunged Him into the bitterness of our sin. Jesus and the tree upon which He hung soaked up our bitterness and transformed it into sweetness of soul. Only Jesus can take our bitterness—our hurt, our pain, our disappointment— and make it a sweet spot in our hearts. His Presence in our lives replaces bitterness with His sweet Living Water.

The transformation of the water was astounding enough, but what came next is the real miracle. The Lord gave a conditional promise of healing:

If you diligently heed the voice of the LORD your God and do what is right in His sight, give ear to His commandments and keep all His statutes, I will put

none of the diseases on you which I have brought on the Egyptians. For I am the LORD who heals you.
(Exodus 15:26)

First, the Lord asks us to listen for His whispers of love, to heed His voice, to give careful thought to His instruction. I pray daily, "Lord, open my ears that I might hear Your voice within me." What precious communion we have. He speaks to us in many ways: through a tender and quiet voice within, through His Word, through His servants—many ways. We only need to listen.

Second, the Lord asks us to *do what is right in His sight.* He wants us to be doers of the Word, not just hearers. You're a servant. I know in my *knower* that you already exhibit an obedient heart. But often, we're so busy doing the work of the Father—doing what is right in His sight—that we mistakenly place the emphasis merely on "doing," rather on doing those things that draw us closer to Him. I love what Beth Moore said in her fabulous Bible study, *A Woman's Heart: God's Dwelling Place:* "Only when we invite the One who hung on that tree to be plunged into our hearts can we begin to know the refreshment of sweet water."[15]

How do we invite Jesus into the broken, bitter places of our heart? It begins with heeding His voice: *"Come to Me, all you who labor and are heavy-laden and overburdened, and I will cause you to rest. [I will ease and relieve and refresh your souls]"* (Matthew 11:28 AMP). I love how *The Message* interprets Matthew 11:28-30:

Jesus said, *"Are you tired? Worn out? Burned out on religion? Come to Me. Get away with Me and you'll recover your life. I'll show you how to take a real rest. Walk with Me and work with Me—watch how I do it. Learn the unforced rhythms of grace. I won't lay anything heavy or ill-fitting on you. Keep company with Me and you'll learn to live freely and lightly."*

Isn't that a perfect description of a weary servant's heart that reeks of bitterness, or at least extreme frustration from endless battles for the sake of righteousness? I can certainly relate. Can you?

Have you ever felt the nudging of the Holy Spirit asking you to come to Him? I don't mean in a generalized way. I mean specifically come to Him to replace what you lack. Matthew 11:28 is one of those verses that may be so familiar to us, it loses its power. We tend to *know* it, but we forget to apply it. Or we put it into a compartment of nice little Scriptures we've memorized, yet we reduce them to clichés. How sad. I know I'm guilty as charged. Been there, done that.

One particularly stressful day, Jesus' words in Matthew came alive for me. We had been unemployed for two years after leaving our previous church. We weren't hastening to the next church, if you know what I mean, and the job market on our beautiful mountain was null and void. On top of everything else, a serious car accident confined David to the bed for several months. Needless to say, I panicked.

For weeks, I heard the Holy Spirit whisper to my heart, "Come to Me, Nan. Come to Me." Over and over, the message remained the same. Oh, it showed up in different places—Scripture, devotions, songs—but the message was the same: "Come to Me." I pushed it (and Him) aside. I was busy. I was hurting. I didn't want to be bothered.

But the Lord pursues His children. He won't let anything separate us from His remarkable love. So He persisted.

Come to Me, Nan.

There it was again. The same tender message resounded within my heart. This time I melted. My resolve was gone. I stopped what I was doing. I walked into my study and knelt by the couch. Closing my eyes, I imagined Jesus sitting on an enormous rock in a gently sloping pasture. I sat at His feet and looked into His eyes. *Lord, I'm obeying You. I'm coming to You for my provision. I'm coming to You for a peaceful mind. I'm coming to You to steady my heart. Thank You, Lord, for asking me to come.*

In that moment, the Lord gave me a vision of what was happening. I saw my heart as a vessel full of dirty water. It was filled to the brim with fear, anxiety, frustration, and anger. It was filthy. There was no room for the goodness of God. In my vision, I watched as Jesus stooped down and held my heart in His hands. Together, we tilted my heart and poured out all of the bitter water. I emptied it at His feet. All of it. No pious, religious talk. No ma'am. Just raw emotion. I poured it all out before Jesus and then a magnificent thing happened. Jesus stood. He raised His hands to the Father and prayed for me.

I gave Him my hardened heart.

Fill me, Lord. Fill me with faith, with confidence and hope, knowing that You are Jehovah-Jireh, the Lord Who Provides. Knowing that You will never leave me nor forsake me. Knowing that Your love never fails. You, Lord, are my peace.

In that moment, my panic subsided. Hope rose within me. Grace covered me like a cozy quilt, protecting me from the enemy's tormenting glare. My bitterness became sweet. My sorrow, unspeakable joy. The anxiety consuming me dissolved into a pool of perfect peace. And my soul found rest. It was amazing.

Jesus said, *"Come to Me, all you who labor and are heavy-laden and overburdened, and I will cause you to rest. [I will ease and relieve and refresh your souls]"* (Matthew 11:28 AMP). Amen? Yes, amen.

Are you thirsty? Have the cares of this world dehydrated your heart? Do you feel like you'll throw up if you have to walk into that church one more time? View the pain in your heart, not as a struggle to endure, but as an inner thirst to be satisfied by an amazing God. In John 7:37-38, Jesus said, *"If anyone thirsts, let him come to Me and drink. He who believes in Me, as the Scripture has said, out of his heart will flow rivers of living water."*

Jesus is pleading, "When you're afraid, come to Me and drink. When you're alone, come to Me and drink. When you're overwhelmed, come to Me and drink."

Why would Jesus use the Living Water as a metaphor for the Holy Spirit? Because, like water, the Holy Spirit can go where we can't go. Think of a cracked sidewalk. If you poured water onto the concrete, the water would find the cracks and seep in. Let's take this same principle and apply it to our hearts. Remember the dirty water we poured out at Jesus' feet earlier? Thank God the bitterness is gone, but what about the source of the filth?

Imagine your heart as a vessel again. This time we're going to fill it with stones, each one representing a struggle or a wound. Are you angry? Put in a stone. Depressed? Add a stone. Do you want to choke a deacon? That's another stone. Let's add a big one for that. Do you get the picture? Maybe you lost a loved one recently, or you're dealing with a prodigal child. Whatever is causing you pain right now—add a stone to your heart for each wound. Now, in your imagination, bow before the Lord and ask Him to pour the Living Water of His precious Holy Spirit over the broken places of your heart. Open your eyes to see, dear sister, open your eyes to see His Living Water flow over, under, and in between every crevice, every dark corner, every broken place, over every stone. His healing touch is restoring, renewing, replacing all the pain with His love. Asaph cried out to God, *"Whom have I in heaven but you? And earth has nothing I desire besides you. My flesh and my heart may fail, but God is the strength of my heart and my portion forever"* (Psalm 73:25-26 NIV). David said, *"My heart says to you, 'Seek his face!' Your face, Lord, I will seek"* (Psalm 27:8 NIV).

Your face, Lord, I will seek. In response to his heart's cry, David was saying, *"Lord, I'm coming."* I love that. To me, it resonates with the richness of relationship. If we can only get it in our *knowers* that the Lord desires relationship with us—a relationship as real as the one we have with our husbands, our children, and our best friends. That's a little hard to wrap our brains around, but it's essential to our healing and to our walking in the purposes He has for us. God also wants us to understand who He is and in that understanding to be still and trust Him.

I love to swing on our porch swing. There I find solitude with the Lord. There He teaches me about Himself. One hot summer day, I learned a life-changing truth. The air felt sticky. Blazing hot. As I rocked back and forth on the swing, the Lord brought something to my attention: the air was still. It seemed as though the whole earth had ceased its striving. No breeze. No movement in the trees. A doe stepped out of the forest near our home, making her way to the creek, but mid-stride, she, too, stopped. Everything was quiet.

I immediately thought of Psalm 46:10: *Be still, and know that I am God.* I thought about the stillness in the air, and I thought about the Lord's instruction to be still. I pondered it and then said, *Yes, Lord. I'm listening. Open my ears to hear You. Open my eyes to see You.* I continued to swing quietly, attentive to the Lord.

A symphony began. In the midst of the quiet came a song. Many songs. The birds of the air sang praise to their Creator. Birds of many colors sang in harmony, filling the air with acclamation of God's glory. It was beautiful. So beautiful. Within moments, a rain shower fell from the heavens. It wasn't a downpour—just a summer shower to replenish the earth. The air cooled. A slight breeze wafted across the porch. The birds continued their song.

I'm learning that when I make my stubborn self sit still—cease striving—and focus on the goodness of the Lord, praise soon rises in my soul. His grace soon falls like rain to replenish my parched spirit.

I sat still and listened to God's voice:

Child, You're learning to walk in My Presence. You're learning to still your restless spirit and concentrate on Me—to focus on Me instead of your problems. That is good. As surely as your stillness comes, the praise will rise. And when the praise rises, My grace will fall. It's a cycle, a pattern, a law of Mine that always holds true. Always. Be still and know that I am God and ready yourself for the praise and grace to follow. Every time. Without fail. I am God. There is no other.

Oh my goodness! Did you catch that? *As surely as your stillness comes, the praise will rise. And when the praise rises, My grace will fall.* Isaiah laid a similar foundation of hope, restoration, and redemption for the faithful remnant of God's people. The prophet's words in Isaiah 51:1-3 speak directly to you and me. May his words comfort you:

Listen to Me, you who follow after righteousness. You who seek the LORD: Look to the rock from which you were hewn, and to the hole of the pit [quarry] from which you were dug. Look to Abraham your Father, and to Sarah who bore you; For I called him alone, and blessed him and increased him. For the Lord will comfort Zion [that's us], He will comfort all her waste places; He will make her wilderness like Eden, and her desert like the garden of the LORD; joy and gladness will be found in it, thanksgiving and the voice of melody.

Let's put this passage in context. May it bless you as much as it has blessed me. During the time of Isaiah, the Babylonians had conquered Judah. King Nebuchadnezzar completely destroyed the temple in Jerusalem and forced the Hebrews into exile again—this time into Babylon.

Think for a moment about the life transition the Israelites experienced. Not only were they held captive, but also they lost their temple to King Nebuchadnezzar's fury. This was huge in their lives. The temple was God's dwelling place among His people. It was their connection to Him, their sacred place of meeting. In their minds, the destruction of the temple eliminated the Presence of God. And on top of that, they were exiled from their homeland. The sweet Presence of God lay in broken shards of memory. How sad. How frightening.

And how tempting. Once again, God's people had rebelled against His righteousness. Over the years, they had adopted foreign gods and cultural practices that insulted the Lord their God. They were forced to face a transition—exile. It disoriented them. What was their identity? Where was their home?

Life transitions disorient us too. They shake us, throw us a curve ball. We find ourselves riding the waves of a turbulent sea of emotions, cresting with faith, and then quickly plummeting to the depths of fear, anger, and all things bad. "When we have no say in the sudden disruptions that life can bring, disorientation is worsened by loss, remorse, confusion, or anger."[16]

"Disorientation is worsened." Isn't that the absolute truth? Life transitions are hard enough, but when they are forced transitions—oh my. Over the years of ministry, David and I have experienced way too many forced transitions that left us rocking and rolling, cresting and plummeting. Until now. Oh, I still get a little seasick, but my life is no longer destroyed because of the whims of man. I'm learning to draw from the River of Living Water, to press in when I can no longer stand. When I hear Jesus call, "Come to Me," I'm learning to run to Him as fast as my little thunder thighs will carry me.

This same reckoning—this remembering who I am and who He is—is what the Lord was (and is) speaking to His children through the prophet Isaiah. Their captivity was about to end (thank you, Cyrus, king of Persia). Chapters 40-66 of Isaiah were written to provide Israel comfort in their return from Babylon and to offer reassurance during their resettling and rebuilding in the city of Jerusalem.[17] Isaiah 40:1 begins this rich promise of restoration for His people, both now and then: *"Comfort, yes, comfort My people!" says your God.* The Hebrew word for "comfort" is *balag*, which means "to brighten up or encourage." That's the meaning we would expect, right? But according to the *Young's Analytical Concordance to the Bible*, comfort means much more.

The Greek word for "comfort" is *parakaleo*, meaning "to call to one's side, to help."[18] The Lord is calling His people to His side once again where He can restore, not only their relationship with Him but also their knowledge of who they are—children of the Most High God. Remember, the Israelites' temple in Jerusalem had been destroyed. They also believed God had forsaken them and forgotten them in their captivity. Listen to the passion behind God's words: "Comfort, yes, comfort my people!" The Creator of the Universe is commanding the prophet Isaiah to comfort His people, to give them hope, to restore them unto Him. In essence, He's saying, "I am with you. I'll restore what has been taken. I'll come alongside you and give you strength for the journey."

That's what He says to us too.

Because of ministry, we're often forced into "exile." We're often taken captive by the enemy as he torments us. We find ourselves drowning in a sea of wretched emotions that try to separate us from the love of God. But *I am persuaded that neither death nor life, nor angels nor principalities, nor powers, nor things present nor things to come, nor height nor depth, nor any other created thing, shall be able to separate us from the love of God which is in Christ Jesus our Lord* (Romans 8:38-39). Nothing—no thing—can separate us from God's love.

The Israelites were learning the same lesson. Let's revisit Isaiah 51:1-3:

> *Listen to Me, you who follow after righteousness, you who seek the LORD: Look to the rock from which you were hewn, and to the hole of the pit from which you were dug. Look to Abraham your father, and to Sarah who bore you; for I called him alone, and blessed him and increased him. For the LORD will comfort Zion, He will comfort all her waste places; He will make her wilderness like Eden, and her desert like the garden of the LORD;*

joy and gladness will be found in it, thanksgiving and the voice of melody.

Again, we hear passion in the Lord's voice as He embraces the hearts of His children: "Listen ... look." Dear sister, can you hear Him longing, pleading, to help you too? He's calling for us to come to Him, to listen to His words of hope, to look at our foundation. The Lord reminded the Hebrew people to consider the rock from which they came. The Lord Himself is our Rock, our Fortress, and our Deliverer. He is in us and we are in Him (John 15:5). God implored them to look at Abraham and Sarah. Abraham was called to follow God. He had no idea where he was going, but he said, "Yes, Lord" (Genesis 12:1-4). Talk about disorientation! Abraham stepped out in faith from the known into the unknown. He stepped out in confidence because he knew the One in whom he had believed. And what about Sarah? Sarah was barren. Her body was tired and old, yet God touched her. From her barrenness came the seed of Israel. Her desert places were filled with joy; her wastelands restored to the glory of God. Oh my goodness. Yes! The Lord is calling to us as He called to the children of Israel. Can you hear Him? Can you see Him in your midst?

I love the Lord's promise not only to comfort and to come alongside and help us, but also to make our impossible waste places beautiful and full of new growth. He promises to make our desert places as glorious as the Garden of Eden. Instead of vegetative growth, this Eden is filled with praise and thanksgiving. Its thirst is quenched from the River of Living Water running deep within. Pure water. Clean. Holy. Water flowing over and under the stones that have wounded us.

Come. Won't you drink from His cup with me? Healing awaits you. Restoration. Hope. A heart-song born of adversity is beautiful indeed. A heart-song born of faith-wrenching grief plants its roots in streams that flow from the throne of God—streams that will never run dry, streams that merge our bitter waters with the cross of Jesus and turn them sweet. But to learn the melody, we must sit at Jesus' feet and allow Him to teach us. We must answer His call with an expectant, "Lord, I'm coming!"

God is calling us to look past the struggles and see His face, hear His voice, and recognize His Presence. He's calling us to Himself. Healing requires our cooperation. Will you allow the Lord to complete the work of healing He has begun in you? Let it go. Pour out the pain and frustration at His feet. He's holding a cup of Living Water for you. Will you take it? Will you drink from His cup?

> Then we turned back and set out toward the wilderness along the route to the Red Sea, as the LORD had directed me. For a long time we made our way around the hill country of Seir. Then the LORD said to me, "You have made your way around this hill country long enough; now turn north." (Deuteronomy 2:1-3 NIV)

Turn northward. Step out of the wilderness. The wilderness in which you've been wandering has a pathway that leads northward toward the throne of God.

I once asked the Lord about this Scripture. "What do You mean, Lord? How do I find my way out of this dismal place?"

In My Presence, He answered. *In My Word, conversing with Me, singing My praise. I long to be with you, child, but you must be intentional about spending time with Me. You can stand in My river all day long, but unless you drink of its Water, you will die of thirst. Turn northward toward my throne. I'm holding the cup.*

Remember, the pains of your heart aren't struggles you must endure. Your pain represents an inner thirst that can be satisfied only by an amazing God. Jesus is calling, *Come to Me, child. Come to Me and find your rest.*

Promises for the Peril of Thirst

"The poor and needy seek water,
but there is none, their tongues fail for thirst.
I, the LORD, will hear them;
I, the God of Israel, will not forsake them.
I will open rivers in desolate heights,
and fountains in the midst of the valleys;
I will make the wilderness a pool of water,
and the dry land springs of water."
~ Isaiah 41:17-18

They shall neither hunger nor thirst,
neither heat nor sun shall strike them;
For He who has mercy on them will lead them,
even by the springs of water He will guide them ...
Sing, O heavens! Be joyful, O earth!
And break out in singing, O mountains!
For the LORD has comforted His people,
and will have mercy on His afflicted.
~ Isaiah 49:10, 13

They wandered in the wilderness in a desolate way;
They found no city to dwell in.
Hungry and thirsty, their soul fainted in them.
Then they cried out to the LORD in their trouble,
and He delivered them out of their distresses.
And He led them forth by the right way,

that they might go to a city for a dwelling place.
Oh, that men would give thanks to the LORD for His goodness,
and for His wonderful works to the children of men!
For He satisfies the longing soul,
and fills the hungry soul with goodness.
~ Psalm 107:4-9

CHAPTER EIGHT

THE SECRET PLACE BENEATH HIS WINGS

The Perils of Anxiety and Fear

THE OAK ROCKING chair embraced me with its soothing motion. I rubbed the end of the armrest, lulling my anxious thoughts into an exhausted stillness. My tissue was tattered and torn from the insistent torrent of tears.

I sighed.

Lord, I need You. I feel like my world is collapsing around me. Everything is so fragmented. Nothing makes sense. I don't understand why everything is a struggle. Why, Lord? My heart is weary; my spirit is drained. Fill my cup with You. I choose You, Lord. I choose You over everything the world has to offer. You're my source of strength, my peace. Draw me close to You.

A refreshing breeze calmed me as I rocked and hummed "The Old Rugged Cross." Something about that old hymn stirs my spirit: "So I'll cherish the old rugged cross, till my trophies at last I lay down; I will cling to the old rugged cross, and exchange it someday for a crown."[19] Over and over, the words flowed like liquid love through my parched spirit. I pictured the cross on which Jesus died for me so that I would never be alone, so that I would always have hope and assurance. I thought about the purpose of the cross—how Jesus' death and resurrection made it possible for me to approach the throne of God, to know the Most High God. I closed my eyes and could see His face. He looked at me, pleading with me to embrace His sacrifice and to understand the depth of its meaning.

Lord, show me. Help me understand.

Deep within my spirit, I heard Him whisper:

Nan, I am with you. I am your hiding place. In Me. In My Presence. My dear child, you have been given the redemptive work of the cross. Walk in that work. Live in that grace. My Presence is with you. All that I am is within you. Let My Spirit comfort you, console you, soothe your anxious heart. Let Me give you rest. You're not alone in your fear, in your pain. No. I am with you now and forever. Child, open your eyes and see Me. Know Me. Love Me. For it is in Me that you live and move and have your being. In Me. I am your hiding place.

My body relaxed. Tension and frustration oozed out of me like infection from a wound. The Presence of

God touched me and made me whole again. He opened my eyes to see and know Him on a deeper level. This is another one of the mysteries reserved for the child of God who dares to press in and *know* Him. You too have been given the redemptive work of the cross, and His Presence is with you as He is with me. The battle is fierce, but His grace is sufficient. His secret place is stocked with abundant grace. Generous love and comfort are stored there. Safety. Security. Let the Holy Spirit take you to the secret place of the Most High God. It's a refuge when life and ministry become overwhelming. There's something very comforting about the touch of His wing.

Are you familiar with Psalm 91? Read the entire psalm. It's powerful. For the sake of this chapter, though, we will look at the first two verses. I pray that this revelation knowledge will change your life too.

He who dwells in the secret place of the Most High shall abide under the shadow of the Almighty. I will say of the LORD, "He is my refuge and my fortress; My God, in Him I will trust" (Psalm 91:1-2). In these two verses, three different names for God are used to express three of His attributes. This is important to note because God is so awesome. He is full of wonder and beyond comprehension. Each name gives us a glimpse into the secret place reserved for us, if we'll open our eyes to see and our ears to hear. These names establish how mighty, yet how loving and merciful, the Lord really is.

The first name the psalmist used was *El Elyon*—the Most High God. *El Elyon* is the sovereign ruler over the entire universe. He's in control. He has dominion over all things. Next was *El Shaddai*—the Almighty God. *El Shaddai* is the all-sufficient One. He's our protector, the caregiver. When we need to be held, *El Shaddai* holds us. *El Shaddai* (Almighty God) is the One who made the covenant with Abraham and said, *"I will establish My covenant between Me and you and your descendants after you in their generations, for an everlasting covenant, to be God to you and your descendants after you"* (Genesis 17:7). He's our life sustainer. The third name of God used in these two verses was *Elohim*—the God of gods, the exalted One. *Elohim* is the Creator of the Universe. Now, let's interject these Hebrew names of God into verses one and two: *He who dwells in the secret place of* El Elyon *shall abide under the shadow of* El Shaddai. *I will say of the Lord, "He is my refuge and my fortress;* Elohim, *in Him I will trust."*

And now—are you ready? Let's put it all together as a paraphrase: He who dwells in the secret place of *El Elyon*, the Most High God, the sovereign ruler of the universe, the One who knows everything that comes my way—if I dwell in His secret place, then that means I'll abide, or live, under the shadow of *El Shaddai*, the Almighty God, the One who holds me when I'm frightened. I'll live under the shadow of the One who holds me when I need comfort, the One who gives me life. I'll live under His shadow because I dwell with the Most High God. And I'll say of the Lord, "You are my refuge and my fortress, *Elohim*—the One True God, the exalted One. In You will I trust."

I'm convinced the secret place of the Most High God is actually the shadow of His Presence. Metaphorically, the secret place is found beneath the shadow of His wing. The

Scriptures contain many references to the Lord's wing. Psalm 57:1 reads, *Be merciful to me, O God, be merciful to me! For my soul trusts in You; And in the shadow of Your wings I will make my refuge, until these calamities have passed by.* When David wrote these words, he was hiding in a cave because Saul was hunting him. Talk about a calamity! David's enemy was in hot pursuit. His enemy's name was Saul; our enemy's name is Satan. Psalm 61:3-4 reads, *For You have been a shelter for me, a strong tower from the enemy. I will abide in Your tabernacle forever; I will trust in the shelter of Your wings.*

As I tried to understand what the Lord was showing me, He led me to Ezekiel 16:8: *"When I [the Lord] passed by you again and looked upon you, indeed your time was the time of love; so I spread My wing over you and covered your nakedness. Yes, I swore an oath to you and entered into a covenant with you, and you became Mine," says the LORD God.* Isn't that interesting? This verse is in the middle of a prophetic message about God's unfailing love for Jerusalem. The children of God had lapsed into idolatry. They were no longer worshiping the One True God. In Ezekiel 16, the Lord is reminding the Israelites of their covenant heritage. The image here is one of the Lord searching for a people, finding them, and claiming them as His own, as in a marital covenant. He spread His wing over them and covered their nakedness. His wing. I wondered why.

My research led me to Ruth 3:7-9:

And after Boaz had eaten and drunk, and his heart was cheerful, he went to lie down at the end of the heap of grain; and she [Ruth] came softly, uncovered his feet, and lay down. Now it happened at midnight that the man was startled, and turned himself; and there, a woman was lying at his feet. And he said, "Who are you?" So she answered, "I am Ruth, your maidservant. Take your maidservant under your wing, for you are a close relative [redeemer]."

Several commentaries explain that when Ruth asked Boaz to take her under his wing, she was actually asking him to spread the corner of his garment over her. In the ancient Middle Eastern world, the practice of casting a garment over a person indicated a claim for marriage.[20] My spirit stirred within me as I read those words. The Lord's wing is the hem of His garment covering the nakedness of our sins and claiming us as His bride. Oh my! My eyes tear up as I think of His love and the intricacies of His Word. When He spread His magnificent wings—the hem of His garment—over us, He became our God and we became His people. The covenant allows us to come into His Presence. Always. He promised never to leave us nor forsake us. We became His special treasure. And we can enter His secret place whenever we need the touch of our Redeemer.

In fact, when we learn to dwell there, we find ourselves living in the shadow and shelter of His wing. Shadows are dark, right? Evil is also dark, figuratively speaking, but when we walk closely with the Lord, when we dwell in His Presence, our immediate darkness is but the shadow of His wing, not the evil lurking nearby. Our immediate surroundings are dark because of His shadow. We're sheltered beneath His wing in a place near to His heart. He shelters us there until the calamities pass.

Imagine that you're a wheat farmer. You've worked hard, growing acres and acres of wheat. It's a good living for your family. Your wheat will be ready to harvest in about ten days. It's already dried out—dry enough to burn.

A fast and furious thunderstorm roars through your community. The cloud-to-ground lightning is fierce. It seeks targets to devour. Your grandma's apple tree still stands tall in the field of wheat. Standing alone, its lichen-covered branches tease the lightning. Out of the darkened sky snakes an electrical finger. It makes contact. *Boom!* The apple tree is set ablaze. Flames consume the ancient family heirloom. They lick the dried wheat, igniting it with angry fervor. The storm moves on, but the destruction has just begun. You and your family rush to put out the blaze, but the inferno is too dangerous. You set backfires to save your house and barn, but the wheat is a total loss.

After the fire dies and the embers cool, you and your honey walk hand-in-hand through the carnage. Thoughts of despair rack your mind. How will we feed the kids this winter? Do we have the strength and fortitude to start over? Overwhelmed, you keep walking.

And then it happens. A God-moment.

You come across the charred body of a hen. Your husband uses the toe of his boot and tips the hen over. From beneath her wing run a dozen little diddles—baby chicks! Because the mother hen spread her wings and beckoned her little ones to come, she protected them from the flames. The chicks lived; they survived the calamity. Because the hen was willing to die, her children, who found shelter under her wings, live.

We, dear sister, are the little chicks.

Because Jesus was willing to die, we can run beneath the shadow of our heavenly Father's wing. He's our shelter from the storm. We can experience the refuge of His Presence. His secret place is our haven until the calamity passes by.

A few months ago, I was having an especially difficult day. A deacon's wife had flung false accusations at my husband concerning favoritism and showing partiality in the church. Honestly, we thought we had finally found a peaceful, purpose-driven church. From day one, the church had been different from all the previous ones—in a good way. And then this accusation came out of left field. This lady was very unhappy about the kind of people David's ministry was bringing into the church. Apparently, she had been spending her days wagging her tongue, creating contention throughout the congregation, spreading her rebellion. Her complaint was that David and I were spending so much time with the people who certainly didn't belong in our fine, upstanding church that we didn't have time for our older members. The truth of the matter: we chose not to spend time with her. We were very faithful to the other church members. Her critical spirit was difficult at best and destructive at worst. But she had influence, and, as you know, where there is influence, there is power. This woman was flicking her power and influence around like a June bug on a string, moving incessantly around and through the congregation, drawing attention to her deception. Seriously? I couldn't believe we were going to circle the mountain of ministry upheaval again. We were devastated.

Then I heard the Lord call to me. *Nan, I'm here.*

I'm coming, Lord.

I pictured Jesus with me, reaching out, beckoning me to His secret place. I was so upset and fearful. I knelt before the Lord and poured out my heart. I gave Him all the dirty, bitter water and asked Him to replace it with His precious Living Water. And then I became still and quiet. I was exhausted by the outpouring of emotion, yet I felt strangely peaceful. The silence was refreshing. I felt safe and secure while I rested in His Presence. Even though the enemy taunted and mocked me, I knew I was safe.

After several minutes, I began to encourage myself in the Lord like David did throughout the psalms: *You, Lord, are the great God. You are faithful and true. You are mighty to save. Nothing is too difficult for You.*

The Lord began to refresh my spirit and fill me with hope.

I continued, *Lord, I know the plans You have for us are to give us a future and a hope. You promise to work all things together for our good. You have never left us nor forsaken us, and I know You never will. I love You, Lord.*

Hope and courage surged within me. I was no longer afraid. I got up, took out my Bible, and crawled up on the loveseat. I was reading the Word, thinking about the goodness of the Lord, when something hit my head. I was baffled. I was alone in the house. No one was in the room except me, yet something hit my head.

I got up to find whatever had hit me. I searched around the loveseat and there, lying on the floor, was a giant feather. (No, it didn't fall from heaven.) It was a pheasant feather I had found in the woods a few years previous. I keep it on my bookcase because it reminds me of the shelter of God's wings. The feather had been on my bookcase for over two years. Two years. I started laughing and said, "Only You, Lord. You're so funny."

And He said, *Nan, I will hide you beneath the shadow of My wing until this calamity passes by. You are in My Presence. The darkness you feel is My shadow sheltering you from the enemy. You, my sweet child, have found my secret place.*

God longs to impart the knowledge of His Presence to you—to get it in your *knower*, not just your head. Gaining the understanding that God is with me always has loosed the chains that kept me bound. Understanding that in Him I live and move and have my being has changed my life (Acts 17:28, paraphrased). He has opened my eyes to see Him all around me—in the whispering pines swaying to His touch, in the thunderhead looming overhead, and in the baby bluebirds nestled in their pine-needle-and-twig bed, mouths open waiting to be filled.

These perceptions and observations come straight from the Word of God. They come from spending time at His feet, listening and conversing. For example, we know that He walks on the wings of the wind (Psalm 104:3), the clouds are the dust of His feet (Nahum 1:3), and He holds the seas in the hollow of His hands (Isaiah 40:12).

He's an amazing God, full of wonder, mighty in power. All of creation declares His glory if we only open our eyes to see. Many times we miss the Lord in our midst because we fail to have our minds stayed on Him. We tend to put Him back in our pretty little box until we need Him. But He's there. Always. We're completely surrounded and immersed in His Presence.

Throughout my Christian walk, the emphasis has been on the Spirit of God dwelling within me. Praise God that He lives within us. Hallelujah! The same power that raised Christ from the dead dwells in us. What an incredible miracle that is. But the life-changer for me, once again, is rooted in John 15:5. Jesus said, *"I am the vine, you are the branches. He who abides in Me, and I in him bears much fruit; for without Me you can do nothing."* Abide in Me and I in you. There's something wonderful about the word *in* as it's used in this verse: *"Abide in Me and I in you."*

One way Satan has deceived us is to cause us to overlook the fact that we are in Jesus, that we dwell within the Spirit of God, completely surrounded by His love. This deception affects how much we trust God. Why? In an odd sort of way, we're filtering God's power through our own limitations. We're seeing the Lord through our fragile vessel rather than seeing Him as the magnificent God that He is, apart from us. When we open our eyes to see Him fully—outside of ourselves—we begin to grasp the very essence of who He is. We begin to understand why we can run to Him and be safe.

Psalm 139:7-10 speaks of His Presence:

Where can I go from Your Spirit? Or where can I flee from Your Presence? If I ascend into heaven, You are there; If I make my bed in hell, behold, You are there. If I take the wings of the morning, and dwell in the uttermost parts of the sea, even there Your hand shall lead me, and your right hand shall hold me.

In Isaiah 41:10 God says, *"Fear not, for I am with you; Be not dismayed, for I am your God. I will strengthen you. Yes, I will help you, I will uphold you with My righteous right hand."*

Consider this: Psalm 90:1 reads, *Lord, You have been our dwelling place in all generations.* The verse doesn't say the heavens are our dwelling place or we'll live at the foot of His throne. No. This Scripture (and many more like it) tells us the Lord is our dwelling place. He is an actual place of refuge, there beneath the shadow of His wing. His Presence is a place we can run to. Can you see it? Yes, the Lord is Spirit, but He is tangible. We can touch Him with our hearts.

I love Exodus 33:14. *And He [the Lord] said, "My Presence will go with you, and I will give you rest."* The Hebrew word for "rest" as used in this verse is *nu'ach* (noo-ahch), which means "to settle down; to be soothed or quieted; to be secure; to be still; to dwell peacefully."[21]

God's Presence does this. His Presence comforts, settles, soothes, and quiets us. But we must dwell with Him, and we must run to Him as our refuge and hide beneath the shadow of His wing until the calamity passes us by. For *there is no one like the God of Jeshurun [Israel], who rides the heavens to help you, and in His excellency on the* clouds. *The eternal God is your refuge, and underneath are the everlasting arms; He will thrust out the enemy from before you, and will say, "Destroy!"* (Deuteronomy 33:26-27).

I'm learning that the quickest way to hide in the secret place of the Most High is to speak the Name of Jesus. It's that simple. "Jesus ... Jesus." At times in my life, that was all I could say. I couldn't pray. I couldn't see past the mountain before me. Other times I was so weakened by sorrow and despair I had no fight in me. I had no ability to run to Him. But when I called out His beautiful Name—the Name above all names—*Jesus,* He ran to me and spread His wing so I could lie down and rest. Can you see that beautiful image? The Lord always responds to the sound of His Name. To repeat: when we're too weak and overwhelmed to run to Him, we can call out the Name of Jesus, and He'll run to us. Oh, what a glorious thought.

Let's return to Psalm 91:1-2. *He who dwells in the secret place of the Most High shall abide under the shadow of the Almighty. I will say of the LORD, "He is my refuge and my fortress; My God, in Him I will trust."* I'm reminded of a recent journal entry where the Lord clearly showed me that He's my fortress. He revealed this lesson to me in the garden:

I hit the fallow ground hard with the hoe. Dirt sprang up with every blow. Weeds surrendered to my hand. And I watered the earth with my tears.

Unimaginable anguish gripped me. Life had been coming at us hard lately. Not only us, but those we love. It felt as though everything was tumbling out of control. We have a very uncertain future. Someone we cherish tried to take his life. False, evil accusations from someone we considered to be a sister in the Lord attacked the very core of who we are. This avalanche has consumed us within a three-day stretch.

This morning, I didn't know if I could survive the enemy's assault.

As the day went on, I attacked the garden space with angry fervor. I pounded the earth with my hoe, weeping with gut-wrenching sobs. I ranted and raved about everything. About nothing. I caught myself proclaiming to no one but the spider clinging to the neighboring milkweed, "Everybody leave me alone." When I'm in this much pain, I cocoon. I go into my cocoon and build up walls of safety around myself. I build a fortress all about me. So leave me *alone*!

As sure as the sunrise, at that moment, I heard the Lord say, "Nan, I *am* your fortress and your refuge. It is *in* Me that you live and move and have your being. In Me."

Well, okay then. That quickly got my attention. Stop for a minute and let this truth sink in, especially in light of what we've been learning about His secret place.

Notice that once again the Lord brought Acts 17:28 to my attention: *in Him we live and move and have our being.* Isn't that remarkable? If only we could get that into our *knowers.* We're surrounded and immersed in God's Presence when we walk closely with Him as His child. What I perceived as a cocoon, a place where no one could find me, a place of solitude, a place to collect my thoughts and survive— my cocoon—was actually exchanged for His secret place at the time of my salvation. I no longer need to build my own place of safety from the world. I am *in* Him. And so are you.

The psalmist described the Lord as his refuge and his fortress. The Hebrew word for "refuge" is *machseh* (mahch-seh), which means "a shelter, refuge, protection, fortress; a hope; a place of trust; a shelter from the storm."[22] The Lord is a *place* of trust. A secret place. A fortress. I love the imagery these words evoke. Do you recall Psalm 57:1? *Be merciful to me, O God, be merciful to me! For my soul trusts in You; And in the shadow of Your wings I will make my refuge, until these calamities have passed by.* King David discovered his *machseh*—a place of trust and refuge—beneath the shadow of the Lord's wing. Picture David nestling under God's wings for refuge like a baby bird hides itself under its parent's wing or like the baby chicks that hid beneath the mother hen's wings until the fire passed them by. The shadow of His wing is the shadow of His Presence—the secret place of the Most High God.

Oh, how great the Father's love for His children! Can we fathom it? Can we awaken our hearts and allow His love to swell within us like ocean waves? Is it possible to open our ears and hear His sweet whispers of affirmation and His shouts of delight simply because we are His? Yes. Yes, it's possible. Zephaniah 3:17 reads, *The LORD your God in your midst, the Mighty One, will save; He will rejoice over you with gladness, He will quiet you with His love, He will rejoice over you with singing.* The Lord delights over us with irresistible joy. The Hebrew word for "rejoice" is *gil* (geel), which "suggests dancing with joy, or leaping for joy because the verb originally meant to spin around with intense motion."[23]

God celebrates His love for us. Shouldn't we do the same? When we call out to Him in our distress, when we run to Him and hide within His mighty Presence—at those times His Father's heart swells to overflowing with love for us. In the shadow of His wing, He quiets us with His love. In the shadow of His wing, He lulls His child to peaceful sleep. The anguish dissipates. The fear is cast out. And the tears cease.

I may not want to praise God for my circumstances, but I can always praise Him for Who He is. I can always celebrate His goodness and His love. A heart filled with praise is a heart that can rest in her Father's love—it's a heart that beats in the secret place beneath the shadow of His wing.

Promises for the Perils of Anxiety and Fear

And David said to his son Solomon,
"Be strong and of good courage, and do it;
do not fear nor be dismayed,
for the LORD God—my God—will be with you.
He will not leave you nor forsake you,
until you have finished all the work
for the service of the house of the LORD."
~ 1 Chronicles 28:20

"Fear not, for I am with you;
Be not dismayed, for I am your God.
I will strengthen you, Yes, I will help you,
I will uphold you with My righteous right hand.
Behold, all those who were incensed
against you shall be ashamed and disgraced;
They shall be as nothing,
and those who strive with you shall perish.
You shall seek them and not find them—
those who contended with you.
Those who war against you shall be as nothing,
as a nonexistent thing.
For I, the LORD your God, will hold your right hand,
saying to you, 'Fear not, I will help you'."
~ Isaiah 41:10-13

Moses said, *"Be strong and of good courage,*
do not fear nor be afraid of them;
for the LORD your God,
He is the One who goes with you.
He will not leave you nor forsake you."
~ Deuteronomy 31:6

CHAPTER NINE

STAND BY YOUR MAN

The Peril of a Strained Marriage

YEARS AGO, AN older Christian woman helped me understand the *S* word: submission. As I prayed about how to approach this chapter, my dear friend's explanation came to mind. Although chapter nine isn't about submission, it is about being the helpmates God has called us to be.

Picture a table. Its components are the top and four legs. In God's law, imagine the husband as the tabletop and the wife as the table legs. The tabletop is above the legs, but without the legs, the tabletop would only be a slab of lumber. The tabletop couldn't function as a table. The same is true of the table legs. They're beneath the table, but without the tabletop, the legs would be four pieces of useless lumber. Neither could function as the carpenter intended without the other. They're of equal importance—just different roles. So it is in a marriage. The husband is placed above the wife, but without the wife undergirding him, he can't fulfill God's purposes for his life. Without the husband assuming his role as the leader in the marriage, the wife can't function in the role God has purposed for her. (Okay. I heard you say, "Awww.") Isn't that incredibly beautiful? I know, right?

Keep this image in the forefront of your mind as we journey through the insights the Lord has given me concerning how to stand by our men when their life's purpose has been ripped from them. I'm not discounting your pain. Heaven forbid! But we must agree on this: our husbands are the ones who ultimately answer yes or no to God's instruction to pastor. They're the tabletops—the leaders. Our job is to undergird them in such a way that they can step into the future with confidence in the One in whom they have believed. I'm praying that you'll receive a warm, fuzzy wave of love and purpose as we address these issues.

Ephesians 5:33 gives us the greatest instruction of all: *and let the wife see that she respects her husband.* Respect—such a simple word. Really? According to *Roget's 21st Century Thesaurus,* comparable words for respect are "admiration, appreciation, consideration, esteem, honor, have a high opinion of, and look up to."[24] I asked David about the effect my respect for him has. He told me this: when I show that I respect him, it gives him the confidence he needs to make decisions concerning us. It gives him the confidence to walk in faith and obedience to the Lord because I trust his ability to hear the Lord. And ladies, don't assume your husband knows that you respect him, just as we don't want to assume our husband loves us. We want him to tell us, to show us loud and clear. We need to know in our *knower* that he loves and cherishes us. Respect is the same way for our husband. He needs us to tell him how much we appreciate his leadership. He needs for us to express our confidence in his ability to find God's guidance. And he needs to know that we're praying for him.

In our region of the country, parsonages are becoming a thing of the past. But one church we pastored still used the parsonage as part of the pastor's package. It was literally on the church property, making it very convenient until trouble came. As "ugly" reared its head, we realized that not only were we about to lose our church—our livelihood—but also we were about to lose our home.

The pressure on my man was enormous.

David has a pastor's heart the size of a mountain. He shepherds his flock, cares for them, comforts them, and protects them. When trouble comes to the church, he doesn't watch out for his own back—every decision he makes is for the sake of the church. I've watched him lay down his life for a church many times. On this particular occasion, his ability to hear the Lord's instruction was crucial to our entire future. He had to do what was right for the congregation, but he also had to make sure we didn't end up on the street.

We spent a lot of time communicating honestly and openly. It's important that emotions are shared freely, with authenticity. A crisis is not the time to accuse or indicate disappointment. It's definitely not the time for a holier-than-thou attitude. The Lord revealed very clearly to me that, although I was in considerable emotional pain,

David's burden was much greater. David was shouldering my burdens as well as his own. I needed to realize that. I asked the Lord how I could help him withstand the fire.

Deep within my soul, I heard the Lord say:

Be there unconditionally for him—a safe haven where he can be himself, where he can show his weaknesses and his fears. He needs for you to speak praise over him and trust. Feed his manhood by letting him know that you respect him—that you have confidence in his ability to lead, to pastor, and to hear My voice. Speak lavishly of your love for him.

And that's what I did. I intentionally built up my husband with words of praise. Please don't misunderstand. Your pain during these times is as real and important as your husband's—you need to be loved, comforted, and reassured too. Express that to him, but then get back to your job of undergirding your man. Consider the image of the tabletop and legs, and understand your role in the trial. I'm learning that when we accept and walk within the purposes God has designed for us—especially within the realms of ministry—we can survive the fire with both our marriage and our sanity intact.

I've tried to live by this principle through all of these years of marriage and ministry. Sometimes I have to bite my tongue and surrender the emotions lapping at my heart to the One who alone can give me sufficient grace to survive the moments. And sometimes, unfortunately, I fail. But you know what? When I deny myself because of the Lord's instruction and focus on the needs of my husband, my wounds heal much quicker. I can't do this in my own strength and neither can you, but with God all things are possible. He'll instill within you the assurance of His Presence. He'll shine His light on the purposes for undergirding your husband, and you'll reap the benefits of a stronger marriage and a life driven by God's purposes. The Lord is free to work within a life surrendered completely to Him. Just watch. He'll work many miracles for you and your husband as you surrender to Him.

Prayer is absolutely the single most important thing we can do to undergird our man. I'm talking specific, directed, intentional prayer—the gut-wrenching kind. Prayer benefits our husband, for sure, but through prayer the Lord instructs us too; through prayer, the Lord grants us discernment into what our husband is going through. Prayer enables us to see into his heart and view the problems through his eyes. At times, it's difficult to understand where our husbands are coming from, what they're feeling, and why they're handling the ministry in a particular way. I know. I get it. But remember, our husbands have a different role to play. He's the tabletop, the leader. He's the provider and the protector. He's a man, for goodness sake! We all know they think differently than women do.

I love what Stormie Omartian said in her book, *The Power of a Praying Wife*: "Your prayers can help cast away discouragement and keep it from taking hold. It can help your husband to hear and cling to God's revelation. It can cause him to live his life on purpose."[25] Do you see how the

Lord wants to use us in this process? Can you sense how honoring our husbands with our prayers honors the Lord above all things? That realization drives me to overcome the evil one. I pray you'll have the same response.

Here's a secret: when our expectations are realistic, grace toward the one we love flows much easier. Each of us knows that our godly man really isn't holy 24/7, right? We know he can lose his temper. We know he gets aggravated and wants to throw in the towel. We also know that even this precious man of God journeys through wilderness times when he goes through the motions of a faith-walk, but he isn't really pressing into Jesus. Can I get an amen? He's human, yes? Yes. Well, guess what? I've done some digging on this subject and discovered that our heroes of faith—the ones we place high on the pedestal of admiration—those guys were human too.

Take Moses, for instance. We all love Moses. He did the impossible many times simply because God asked him to, and he dared to believe God. Do you realize that Moses experienced frustration about his calling that would rival our frustration any day of the week? Let's look at Numbers 11:5-6, 10-15:

> "We [the Israelites] remember the fish which we ate freely in Egypt, the cucumbers, the melons, the leeks, the onions, and the garlic; but now our whole being is dried up; there is nothing at all except this manna before our eyes!" ... Then Moses heard the people weeping throughout their families, everyone at the door of his tent; and the anger of the LORD was greatly aroused; Moses also was

displeased. So Moses said to the LORD, "Why have You afflicted Your servant? And why have I not found favor in Your sight, that You have laid the responsibility of all these people on me? Did I conceive all these people? Did I beget them, that You should say to me, 'Carry them in your bosom, as a guardian carries a nursing child', to the land which You swore to their fathers? Where am I to get meat to give to all these people? For they weep all over me, saying, 'Give us meat, that we may eat.' I am not able to bear all these people alone, because the burden is too heavy for me. If You treat me like this, please kill me here and now—if I have found favor in Your sight—and do not let me see my wretchedness!"

Don't you love that? I laugh every time I read it. Can't you hear Moses saying, "Hey God! These are Your children, not mine! I can't handle them another minute, not one. So take me outta here 'cause I'm done."

Elijah had a similar experience when he was fleeing from Jezebel. Israel had been seduced into Baal worship because of Jezebel. A drought had fallen on the land creating a famine, so the Lord sent Elijah to tell the Israelites and King Ahab that their idolatry was the source of the problem. Elijah, a prophet of God, had called for a showdown between the 450 prophets of Baal and the Lord. The contest took place on Mount Carmel with all of Israel present so they could see the error of their ways. The challenge involved two altars, two sacrifices, and a call for the sacrifice to be accepted by either Baal or the One True God. For six hours, the prophets of Baal cried out to their god with no response—they even cut themselves with knives so their blood would get Baal's attention. But nothing happened.

Then it was Elijah's turn. First, he repaired the altar of the Lord that was broken down. Next, he took twelve stones representing the twelve tribes of Israel and used them to build the altar before the Lord. The Israelites were instructed to place wood and the sacrificial bull on the altar. Then they were told to fill pots with water and pour it on the sacrifice and the wood three times. There was so much water that it ran all around the altar and filled the trench. Elijah said:

> "LORD God of Abraham, Isaac, and Israel, let it be known this day that You are God in Israel and I am Your servant, and that I have done all these things at Your word. Hear me, O LORD, hear me, that this people may know that You are the LORD God, and that You have turned their hearts back to You again." (1 Kings 18:36-37)

The consuming fire of the Lord fell, accepting the sacrifice and even licking up the water in the trenches. *Now when all the people saw it, they fell on their faces; and they said, "The LORD, He is God! The LORD, He is God!"* (v. 39). Afterward, the prophets of Baal were seized and killed. Elijah said to Ahab, *"Go up, eat and drink; for there is the sound of abundance of rain"* (v. 41).

When Jezebel heard of the death of her prophets and the humiliation of her god, she sent a message to Elijah:

he would be hunted down and killed. So Elijah ran for his life. Do you remember our discussion of Elijah from chapter six? *But he himself [Elijah] went a day's journey into the wilderness, and came and sat down under a broom tree. And he prayed that he might die, and said, "It is enough! Now, Lord, take my life, for I am no better than my fathers!"* (1 Kings 19:4).

What? Elijah is so despondent he wants to die? Yes. He's human. A few verses earlier, he was full of faith and proclaiming, *"I am Your servant, and I have done all these things at Your word. Hear me, O Lord, hear me, that this people may know that You are the Lord God, and that You have turned their hearts back to You again."* Now he wants to die. He's tired of the battle. Elijah—the mighty prophet of God, worker of incredible miracles—is riding a roller coaster of faith. Should we expect any less of our mighty men of God? I think not. Expectations must be realistic.

David gives us a perfect example of realistic expectations in Psalm 62:

For God alone my soul waits in silence; from Him comes my salvation. He only is my Rock and my Salvation, my Defense and my Fortress, I shall not be greatly moved.

How long will you set upon a man that you may slay him, all of you, like a leaning wall, like a tottering fence? They only consult to cast him down from his height [to dishonor him]; they delight in lies. They bless with their mouths, but they curse inwardly. Selah [pause, and calmly think of that]!

My soul, wait only upon God and silently submit to Him; for my hope and expectation are from Him. He only is my Rock and my Salvation; He is my Defense and my Fortress, I shall not be moved. With God rests my salvation and my glory; He is my Rock of unyielding strength and impenetrable hardness, and my refuge is in God!

Trust in, lean on, rely on, and have confidence in Him at all times, you people; pour out your hearts before Him. God is a refuge for us (a fortress and a high tower). Selah [pause, and calmly think of that]! (vv. 1-8 AMP)

I love how King David encourages himself in the Lord. It's easy to see the battle—the frustration he's experiencing. Right in the middle of reminding himself how great God is, David is sidetracked into how aggravating it is to be maligned by lying lips and backstabbers. This ministers to me.

King David is no different than we are.

He's no different than our husbands.

Psalm 62 reminds all of us that only in God are our expectations realistic. He, alone, is our hope. Our refuge. Our Rock. We must put our trust in Him and not in people. We don't need to preach this to our husbands. (David says I preach to him sometimes. Sigh.) But what a wonderful way to show our husband that he shares his frustrations with good company.

It's so easy for our men to feel like failures. Why? Our husbands shoulder a tremendous amount of responsibility—they're the tabletops, the leaders. That's why it's so important for us to clearly express our respect for them and help our husbands maintain realistic expectations of themselves.

In addition to prayer and respect, it's vital that we keep our husband's divine call ever before him—again, not in preachy tones, but bathed in love, admiration, and respect. Proverbs 29:18 reminds us that *where there is no vision [no redemptive revelation of God], the people perish* (AMP). Nothing will destroy God's vision and purpose for our lives faster than being removed from a pastorate, especially because of church politics. Talk about a vision-killer. When we walk in God's vision, and not our own, we typically don't know all of the specifics, but we do have a general direction—one step at a time. If our man stops walking in faith because he's shutting down from pastoral abuse, he's reluctant to take those steps. If he's not walking in faith, then he's not walking in the knowledge that something good is in his future. Satan steps in and fills his mind with thoughts of failure and doubt, turning his thoughts inward. When our men lose their hope of a future and purpose, you'll surely watch them die a slow death in front of you.

Consider something else Stormie Omartian said:

Even the most spiritual man can get overtired, burned out, beaten down, distanced from God, confused about who he is and why he is here, and lose his vision for the future. He can misplace his sense of purpose and become overwhelmed and hopeless because of it. If he loses sight of his dreams and forgets the truth about himself and his situation, he can end up believing destructive lies about his future.[26]

Dear sister, this is where we undergird our man.

Ask God to give you creative and sensitive ways to restore vision to your husband when it has been lost. The Lord can give him hope to dream again, reassurance that his future rests in God's purposes and His plans. He can restore your man's drive and the knowledge of who he is in Christ. Do you know where this takes us? This sends us right back to the *R* word: Respect. When we concentrate on building our husband's self-esteem through respect, admiration, and unconditional love, he stops building walls. When he stops building walls, he'll open his heart to hear from God.

How can we do this? How about invading his man-cave? I don't mean rearranging and making it comfortable for your girly-self. I mean sit and watch a game because it's important to him. Fix him some popcorn and Coke (or Mountain Dew at our house), put on his favorite team jersey, and yell at the television. I'm serious. He'll love it. Or, how about watching one of those "guy" movies? Ugh. I hate them, but I watch those horrid shoot-em-up conspiracy crime thrillers so I can be with my man. I don't like the movie, but I love David. When I give myself to him in this manner, he knows he's important to me. When a man is hurting, this is huge.

Look for opportunities to leave a note for him. Let it be one of love, but also include an encouraging Scripture passage—maybe one like Isaiah 43:1-3—something that reminds him that he is God's special treasure. Or, write something silly that only you and your honey will get. Hide the notes in his underwear drawer. Stuff one in a bag of his favorite potato chips. Send him on a scavenger hunt that leads him to you out on the back deck with a cup of coffee, James Taylor playing in the background, a couple of candles—you know, create a quiet oasis in the harsh realities of ministry. Be creative. Knowing that you love him and believe in him goes a long way.

We know how important prayer is. That is, by far, the best way to support our husbands. Of course, tell him you're praying for him, but how about sending him an e-Prayer? If he has an e-mail address, click on it, hit compose, and literally type your prayer as you pray for your man. Not only will he see your heart and respect in action, but also he'll have a reference point whenever he feels overwhelmed or alone. It will melt his heart.

Attune your ear to the Lord's voice. He'll give you creative direction and ideas on how to stand by your man. After all, He knows your man better than anyone.

Serving as a table leg never looked so good, huh?

Promises for the Peril of a Strained Marriage

Paul said, *"I, therefore, the prisoner of the Lord,*
beseech you to walk worthy
of the calling with which you were called,
with all lowliness and gentleness, with longsuffering,
bearing with one another in love,
endeavoring to keep the unity of the Spirit
in the bond of peace."
~ Ephesians 4:1-3

"No weapon formed against you shall prosper,
and every tongue which rises against you
in judgment You shall condemn.
This is the heritage of the servants of the LORD,
and their righteousness is from Me," says the LORD.
~ Isaiah 54:17

And above all things have fervent love for one another,
for "love will cover a multitude of sins."
Be hospitable to one another without grumbling.
As each one has received a gift, minister it to one another,
as good stewards of the manifold grace of God.
~ 1 Peter 4:8-10

CHAPTER TEN

I DIDN'T SEE IT COMING

The Peril of the Unexpected

I FELT THE warm drip of tears pooling on my nightgown as my heart tumbled onto the page. Sweet sister, never could I have seen this coming. Never. Ever.

David and I have experienced amazing love throughout our marriage. We've been a team in everything. In our small mountain community, our names are synonymous with one another. Always. David and Nan. Together.

And now it's over. I've never been so broken. So fragile. So alone. Isn't that ironic? I began this book by exhorting you to realize that somewhere, somehow, someone knows what you're going through. And now I'm the one in need. I need your love and your prayers as I share with you the end of my marriage, at least as I have known it for thirty-one years.

I feel compelled to repeat Stormie Omartian's words from chapter nine:

Even the most spiritual man can get overtired, burned out, beaten down, distanced from God, confused about who he is and why he is here, and lose his vision for the future. He can misplace his sense of purpose and become overwhelmed and hopeless because of it. If he loses sight of his dreams and forgets the truth about himself and his situation, he can end up believing destructive lies about his future.[27]

When I first read those words, I was touched by the harsh reality that our men are just that—men. I was moved by the notion that quite easily and quickly our men of God can change. How foolish of me not to see past the rhetoric and understand that these words represent a very real threat to us, to our husbands, and to the pastorate.

My David has become this man.

Throughout our marriage, I've stood by David in the ways I've encouraged you to stand by your man. Publically and privately, I've shown him great respect. I've loved him unconditionally and undergirded him with my prayers. I've stood by him during our ministry trials, reminding him that God is for us, and He will fight the battle.

And then the unthinkable happened.

A sword of unfaithfulness pierced the shield of faith surrounding David and me. Who wielded that sword? Needy women finding a listening ear? A needy man searching for something that was missing or perhaps trying to fix something that is broken?

I don't.know.

I didn't realize anything was wrong. How could I not see it or sense it? Had I become so buried in my own pain from pastoral abuse that what I thought was extending grace to a quiet and somewhat distant husband was actually not being in tune with his needs?

Again, I don't know. I didn't realize my marriage was in trouble.

We were covered in the blood of Jesus. We were in covenant with God—servants of the Most High. How could our marriage be vulnerable to attack? How? Didn't God owe it to us to guard our home, our hearts—my heart?

But pastors are people too. They sin.

Some days I can barely breathe.

Some days I want revenge.

Most days I simply want it to go away.

But that's like spraying water from a garden hose on a raging wildfire. Something poisonous has grown, something with tendrils that run deep and choke the life out of me and my children.

Oh! My precious children. What would I have done without them? They're all young adults living on their own, yet all of them put their lives on hold and came running when they heard the news. My front lawn became a parking lot, a half-moon of hastily parked cars. As I watched my children's arrival from the front porch, it seemed like they were circling their wagons—running home to protect their momma's heart. I had to smile at their sweetness in the middle of the bitter. For the first month, all three of them stayed with me. In the evening after work, we watched movies. They took turns sitting by me on the couch, holding my hand. What a blessed woman I am. These are the things that keep me going.

For many years, Philippians 4:8 has been one of my favorite verses: *Finally, brethren, whatever things are true, whatever things are noble, whatever things are just, whatever things are pure, whatever things are lovely, whatever things are of good report, if there is any virtue and if there is anything praiseworthy—meditate on these things.* Paul goes on to say that when we think on these things and follow his instructions about letting the Lord know our needs with thanksgiving in our heart, then the God of peace will be with us.

I'm living Paul's instructions out loud now.

I've found them to be true.

When I remember those things that are lovely and pure and worthy of praise—like my children, friends, and family who undergird me in my pain—when I think on those things, I rest in the presence of God and His gift of peace. But if I allow my thoughts to stray, to veer off a little, I travel to a dark place very quickly. Those thoughts can push me to the ground where I curl into a fetal position. Choosing to apply the Word of God keeps me sane. Isn't the Lord, in His infinite wisdom, wonderful?

He sustains me, when I let Him.

He carries me, when I take hold of His hand.

He shelters me, when I run to Him.

Such amazing love.

I will not disgrace my husband in these final pages. Certainly, the grace of God covers my own imperfections. I'm old enough to know that each of us makes multiple choices every day, and every choice determines the direction of our path. So I refuse to end this book on a sour note.

My David is a wonderful man. He has impacted many lives with the love of the Lord. He has helped people reconnect with the God of their youth, bringing relief from the chains of religiosity that abound in churches. Yes, he's a good man. But somewhere he got lost. Somewhere a seed of rebellion took root, and its fruit is destroying him.

I've spent a lot of time these past weeks pondering rebellion as a seed. These seeds must be delicate, perhaps clothed in beauty, so we don't recognize their pervasive destruction. When a stiff summer breeze whips across a lawn, wisps of dandelion fluff scatter. Nothing about that delicate white wisp warns us of destruction. We often scatter the seeds ourselves, blowing on the dandelion globe and making a wish. How naive we are at times! How deceived. Like the dandelion seeds dance through the air to our delight, so the seeds of rebellion swirl about us waiting for fertile soil on which to land, take root, and begin the destructive process.

It's quite simple.

It's quite alarming.

I've heard it said that one dandelion seed will carpet the yard if given a little time. One seed takes root and grows into maturity. The flower looks lovely and innocent at first, but then the beauty withers and it becomes a globe of seeds that scatter and multiply, spreading across the landscape. So it is with rebellion.

Rebellion of the heart is hidden. Unspoken. Like the multitude of dandelion seeds hidden in the beauty of the flower, rebellion may be undetected. It waits—waits until the time of scattering, and then it begins to destroy a life.

Perhaps that happened to my David.

In this book, you've read many stories about our trials in ministry—battles fought in the trenches for the sake of righteousness. David was always very attentive to my needs during those battles—not only my needs, but also the needs of those in the congregation who stood for righteousness. Could it be that each battle created chinks in his armor until a crack appeared, providing entry for something dark and ominous? If David didn't receive healing during these times, but only gave the appearance of healing because he was a man, after all—and we know our men don't want to appear weak—I can begin to make sense of what the Lord is showing me. Think about it.

A battle ensues.

A hurt occurs.

Chink! No healing for himself, only for me and for others. Doubt of and disappointment in the God he serves gain entry. A seed of rebellion could easily enter. And the cycle repeats: Battle. Hurt. *Chink!* No healing. Enter seed of rebellion. And again: Battle. Hurt. *Chink!* No healing. Another seed enters. Battle after battle, seeds of rebellion—born of great hurt—gain entry, and like the pervasive dandelion seeds, they carpet his heart while waiting to mature and destroy a beautiful man.

And yet I believe in redemption. And forgiveness.

I'm struck with thoughts of the woman caught in adultery whose story is told in the gospel of John. Do you remember her? And the stones? And the dirt?

Now early in the morning He came again into the temple, and all the people came to Him; and He sat down and taught them. Then the scribes and Pharisees brought to Him a woman caught in adultery. And when they had set her in the midst, they said to Him, "Teacher, this woman was caught in adultery, in the very act. Now Moses, in the Law, commanded us that such should be stoned. But what do You say?" This they said testing Him, that they might have something of which to accuse Him. But Jesus stooped down and wrote on the ground with His finger, as though He did not hear. So when they continued asking Him, He raised Himself up and said to them, "He who is without sin among you, let him throw a stone at her first." And again He stooped down and wrote on the ground. Then those who heard it, being convicted by their conscience went out one by one, beginning with the oldest even to the last. And Jesus was left alone, and the woman standing in the midst. When Jesus had raised Himself up and saw no one but the woman He said to her, "Woman, where are those accusers of yours? Has no one condemned you?" She said, "No one, Lord." And Jesus said to her, "Neither do I condemn you; go and sin no more." Then Jesus spoke to them again, saying, "I am the light of the world. He who follows Me shall not walk in darkness, but have the light of life." (John 8:2-12)

Have you ever wondered why Jesus wrote in the dirt? I've always wondered about that. In fact, I've heard several people expound their ideas. As I was writing this section and praying about my words, I kept thinking about the account of creation in Genesis. God created man out of the dust of the earth. Dirt. After reading Genesis 2:7, I cross-referenced to Psalm 103:14, which says, *for He knows our frame, He [earnestly] remembers and imprints [on His heart] that we are dust* (AMP). He remembers. The Lord understands us, and He recognizes that, ultimately, we're made of dirt. We're imperfect people living in an imperfect world. We aren't righteous in ourselves. We become righteous only through the blood of Jesus, and until the day we meet our Maker and put on our glorious body, we'll continue to be imperfect. Yes, we're made of dirt—the dust of the earth.

Possibly that's what Jesus was thinking about as He wrote in the dirt, as He faced the adulterous woman's accusers. Perhaps He was disappointed in the woman, maybe even righteously angry that she had chosen to sin in such a blatant, toxic manner. But then, He gathered His thoughts as He wrote in the dirt. He remembered from whence she came, and He felt compassion for her. So He forgave her, telling her to go and sin no more. What a stirring thought!

Perhaps when the sin of my David's adultery came before Jesus, He wrote in the dirt once more, remembering that this special servant of God had also come from the dirt. And in His remembering, maybe Jesus had compassion on David and offered forgiveness as He had offered it to the adulterous woman.

How can I do any less? How can you?

I'm made of dirt too.

I'm learning that forgiveness isn't optional. It isn't a suggestion. It's a commandment. Matthew 6:14-15 reads, *For if you forgive men when they sin against you, your heavenly Father will also forgive you. But if you do not forgive men their sins, your Father will not forgive your sins* (NIV).

I choose forgiveness, although the choice to forgive doesn't necessarily mean reconciliation. I have biblical grounds for divorce, but I also have a biblical requirement to forgive. This knowledge lets me breathe when I feel suffocated by decisions because I don't know what my future holds. I have to take it one step at a time, as do you if you find yourself in the same grievous situation.

Rick Warren's wise words ministered to me: "Forgiveness must be immediate, whether or not a person asks for it. Trust must be rebuilt over time. Trust requires a track record. If someone hurts you repeatedly, you're commanded by God to forgive them instantly, but you're not expected to trust them immediately, and you're not expected to continue allowing them to hurt you."[28] Praise God!

Forgiveness, trust, and reconciliation all at once is more than this little bit of dirt can absorb. But forgiveness alone? Yes, with God's grace. Not easily. Not as quickly as I want to, but with God's help, I will come to a place of forgiveness. Not for David's sake, but for my sake. Anne Lamott wrote, "Not forgiving is like drinking rat poison and then waiting for the rat to die."[29] So true. These past several weeks and months, when I found it impossible to forgive and allowed resentment to grow, my spirit became clogged with that poison. The Living Water of the Lord couldn't flow through me. My body responded with a major fibromyalgia flare. Pain wreaked havoc in my body, I slept for hours and hours, and I couldn't concentrate—all because I had swallowed the poison of an unforgiving spirit.

Please learn from my mistake and find the grace to forgive those who have hurt you. With God's help and through His mercy and grace, I will walk in forgiveness, and I will expel the poison from my spirit. I pray the same for you.

Torrents of tears can still overpower me without warning. For example, I'm working part time at a local restaurant. One Sunday afternoon, an elderly couple came in. The "oneness" of their marriage was visible—words spoken through eyes alone, body language indicating endearment. I was drawn to them—their love. I watched intently as they left the restaurant. Each carried a cane. They held hands, supporting one another, strengthening each other's steps.

It tore me up.

That had been my vision—the one I held in my heart for David and me.

And it had been stolen.

Tears spilled from my eyes as my shoulders trembled. The reminder of my loss was almost too much to bear. But God held me, consoled me, and affirmed me in His love. I'm so thankful our tears are precious to Him. I cried off and on for the next twenty-four hours, grieving the man I've loved for thirty-one years. And then I lay my pain at the foot of the cross, once again begging the One who knows me to help me find my way to forgiveness.

My heart's cry is that you'll never know such brokenness as this.

Statistics indicate otherwise.

"Focus on the Family has reported that we in the United States lose a pastor a day because he seeks an immoral path instead of God's, seeking intimacy where it must not be found. F.O.F. statistics state that 70% of pastors do not have close personal friends, and no one in whom to confide. They also said about 35% of pastors personally deal with sexual sin. In addition, that 25% of pastors are divorced."[30]

Oh my! Who knew?

Pastors are people too. They sin.

I hesitated to quote these statistics because I didn't want to instill fear. If you're feeling the talons of fear, I want you to stop reading and rebuke it in the Name of Jesus. Fear isn't from God. But He does give us a sound mind (2 Timothy 1:7).

I may have become so complacent and comfortable in the security of my marriage that I didn't smell the enemy when he came lurking, seeking whom he could devour (1 Peter 5:8).

Don't make my mistake.

Proclaim the Word of the Lord over your marriage.

Together, pray a hedge of protection around your relationship. Daily.

Pray for discernment when pretty little ladies need a listening ear.

Pray for humility as you speak to your husband when your radar beeps that trouble is near.

Never, ever take your precious man for granted. He's a gift from your heavenly Father, one to be treasured and cared for and prayed over daily. *Father, forgive me for taking my David for granted.*

I want to share something I wrote early in my devastation. The Lord shared a profound truth with me. Although it was the first of many, this lesson broke the first link in the chains wrapped around my spirit:

Hot water showered down across my naked body, my raped soul. Anguish deeper than the deepest pit ravished me. Consumed me. Betrayal had carved a cavernous hole in my heart that only the Lord could fill … if I would let Him.

Salty tears dripped into my mouth with each miserable cry. How could I go on? How could I possibly walk in the path the Lord has called me to—the one of helping Christian women struggling with their faith because life is so hard? The path of encouraging other pastors' wives whose rose-colored glasses of ministry have been shattered?

Ironic, isn't it?

Deep inside me, the Lord whispered, *Healing comes in the giving.*

What? I have nothing left to give, Lord. I am depleted, struggling to survive.

Again He spoke, *Healing comes in the giving.*

His tender words swirled through my mind as I watched the soapy water disappear down the drain. I carried them with me in thought as I dressed, grabbed my coffee, and curled up in a rocking chair. I opened the pages of my devotional, *Streams in the Desert* by L.B. Cowman. Today's devotion began with Psalm 138:8, *The Lord will perfect [complete, fulfill] that which concerns me.* I almost dropped the book.

It went on to say, "There is a divine mystery in suffering, one that has a strange and supernatural power and has never been completely understood by human reason. No one has ever developed a deep level of spirituality or holiness without experiencing a great deal of suffering ... when the suffering has accomplished its blessed ministry ... the pain of the crucifixion has begun to weave itself into a crown ... It is in this experience of complete suffering that the Holy Spirit works many miraculous things deep within our soul. In this condition, our entire being lies perfectly still under the hand of God; every power and ability of the mind, will, and heart are at last submissive; a quietness of eternity settles into the entire soul ..."[31]

Sweet sister, this is true for you too. Whether you're a victim of the horrors of infidelity or whether you find yourself painfully burned by the lonely fires of ministry— healing comes in the giving. May we all determine in our hearts to give to others, to walk in the exhortation of Paul: *Blessed be the God and Father of our Lord Jesus Christ, the Father of mercies and God of all comfort, who comforts us in all our tribulation, that we may be able to comfort those who are in any trouble, with the comfort with which we ourselves are comforted by God. For as the sufferings of Christ abound in us, so our consolation also abounds through Christ* (2 Corinthians 1:3-4).

When the suffering has accomplished its blessed ministry, the pain of the crucifixion begins "to weave itself into a crown." The result? A quietness of eternity settles into the entire soul. That, dear one, is the abundant consolation—a gift from the One who loves us.

Am I enjoying this season of suffering and turmoil?

No.

But is the Lord revealing Himself to me through it all?

Is He reminding me of His eternal purposes?

Yes!

As much as I detest the evil that has invaded my home, I know in my *knower* that the Lord will take the pain and weave it into a miraculous crown for my good and for His glory. Such amazing grace. Our God is a very good God.

I want to share a poem with you written by my friend Marcie Bridges. Marcie sent this poem to me during one of the darkest days of my brokenness. It's written in free verse, which powerfully accentuates the compelling message. I believe you'll find comfort and inspiration in the words of her heart.

Notes of Grace

There is a grace that flows on notes
whispered in love. Floating from
skies that lash and rainbows arc
mysteries we see only in the dark.
You might not feel it, might not
know it. It comes in ragged flashes,
a spark that dies then comes back to
life. It jolts. It beckons. It draws us
toward something we knew deep
down existed but never wanted to
explore. The cavernous hole that
empties into our toes. Grace gently,
softly, releases as red and gold leaves
fill the void of the grass on the lawn.
Hush, hush, settle down. Life is too short
and guilt too long to stay hidden
in the clouds. Grace extends its arms
and soothes the parts that feel too
raw, decayed and dead. Winter is over,
Spring renews and herein lies our
hearts. Our buried secrets. Our ugly
parts. Whispers of love flow down
and grace, yes, grace is there to
pick us up and help us lay our burdens
down.[32]

Beautiful, isn't it? Each time I read it, I'm touched by a different word, a different phrase. I can feel Marcie searching for grace as I've searched for it over the past few months. I'm especially drawn to this portion: "It comes in ragged flashes, a spark that dies then comes back to life. It jolts. It beckons." God's grace is constant like the burning embers of a consuming fire, but sometimes we don't tend to it—sometimes we take it for granted and forget to seek the Giver of grace—and the flames of experiential grace die down. But then God, in His infinite mercy, blows the mighty breath of His love on the embers, and a spark of glorious grace descends once again.

The strangest thing just happened.

David called.

The call was on the heels of an e-mail from him. In the e-mail, he described being at "The Lump," our favorite spot on the Blue Ridge Parkway near our home. It's a giant lump of a hill. From the top, you can see forever across the mountaintops. The Lump is where, on many occasions, the Lord has drawn David to Himself. On this day, David had spent the afternoon there praying, reflecting, self-evaluating. Apparently, it became a very holy moment where the Lord shone His magnificent Light into David's darkness and applied the shed Blood of Jesus.

Finally, he shed tears of remorse and accountability for his actions. Finally, a hint of the man I've loved for thirty-one years. And now I sit here sobbing and sobbing uncontrollably. My emotions erupt like a volcano on a mountaintop spewing lava that consumes the new, tender vegetation.

I don't know what to do with my feelings right now.

I don't know what I feel.

Oh Lord, I give You my heart. Melt me, Lord. Mold me. Use me for Your glory. Open my ears to hear Your whispers of instruction. What is Your will, Lord? You're not a God of confusion, but a God of peace. Thank You for Your peace. Surround me with a hedge of protection to protect me from the spewing lava. Steady my heart, Lord. Help me to be still and remember that You are God.

This next portion may seem insignificant to you, my reader, but it's huge in my mind: David's mom named him after King David in the Bible. King David. His name means "beloved of God." Do you remember what this mighty man of God did? He lusted after Bathsheba, committed adultery with her, and then, to cover up his sin, ordered the murder of her husband. King David was a beloved man of God and he sinned.

My David is a beloved man of God and he sinned. Terribly.

The big question is, "What do I do now?" I'm required to forgive; I'm not required to trust. It's my responsibility to forgive. God is responsible for the outcome. The outcome I desire is that my David would be completely restored in his relationship with the Lord—that he would once again live up to the name, Beloved of God.

I don't know where I fit into the picture because trust is an enormous issue. I'm nowhere close to embracing trust right now. Only God can work that miracle. My focus right now is to press on to the mark of the high calling of Jesus Christ (Philippians 3:14). My focus is on Jesus, the author and finisher of my faith (Hebrews 12:2). My focus is to forgive and pray for the restoration of my husband, whether his restoration involves me or not.

I ask that you pray the same.

Isn't it amazing that the first body of text in this book is Romans 8:31-37? Its truth remains for you and me. I would like to share these verses with you once more. Ponder them. Soak them into your spirit. Live them out loud.

If God be for me, who can be against me?

Moreover whom He predestined, these He also called;
whom He called, these He also justified;
and whom He justified, these He also glorified.
What then shall we say to these things:

If God is for us,
who can be against us?

He who did not spare His own Son, but delivered Him up for us all,
how shall He not with Him also freely give us all things?
Who shall bring a charge against God's elect?

It is God who justifies.
It is Christ who died, and furthermore is also risen,
who is even at the right hand of God,
who also makes intercession for us.

Who shall separate us from the love of Christ?
Shall tribulation, or distress, or persecution, or famine,
or nakedness or peril or sword?
As it is written: "For Your sake we are killed all day long:
We are accounted as sheep for the slaughter."

Yet in all these things we are more than conquerors
through Him who loved us.
Romans 8:31-37

Sweet sister, thank you for holding my heart in yours through the difficult pages of this chapter. I trust you with the devastation found here—the broken pieces of my heart. And I cherish your prayers as I wait on the One who holds my tomorrows.

Promises for the Peril of the Unexpected

You will keep him in perfect peace,
whose mind is stayed on You, because he trusts in You.
~Isaiah 26:3

Jesus said, *"My sheep hear My voice,*
and I know them, and they follow me.
And I give them eternal life, and they shall never perish;
neither shall anyone snatch them out of My hand.
My Father, who has given them to Me, is greater than all;
and no one is able to snatch them out of My Father's hand.
I and My Father are one."
~ John 10:27-30

There are many plans in a man's heart,
nevertheless the LORD's counsel [purpose]—that will stand.
~ Proverbs 19:21

CHAPTER ELEVEN

IF GOD BE FOR ME

I TOSSED AND turned; restlessness governed my sleep. All of my dreams seemed to lead me to the edge of a cliff where I would suddenly jerk and wake up before plummeting to my death. My spirit quaked beneath the burdens of my heart.

About four o'clock in the morning, I felt the Holy Spirit nudging me to get up and pray. I called on the Name of Jesus. Nothing more. I was so worn out from the struggle, I no longer had the words to pray. Our merciful and gracious Lord led me to Isaiah 50:

> *The Sovereign LORD has given me an instructed tongue,*
> *to know the word that sustains the weary. He wakens me*
> *morning by morning, wakens my ear to listen like one*
> *being taught … Who among you fears the LORD and*
> *obeys the word of his servant? Let him who walks in the*
> *dark, who has no light, trust in the name of the LORD*
> *and rely on his God.* (Isaiah 50:4, 10 NIV)

Isaiah refers to God as the Sovereign Lord. *Roget's 21st Century Thesaurus* lists the following synonyms for *sovereign*: authority, absolute, commanding, effectual, guiding, highest, majestic, reigning, ruling, and supreme.[33] God wanted to teach me something about His character. He instructed me to add some of these words as adjectives in front of His Name: Absolute Lord, Effectual Lord, Guiding Lord, Supreme Lord, Reigning Lord.

Okay, Lord, You have my attention.

Next I looked up Isaiah 50:10 in *The Amplified Bible:*

Who is among you who [reverently] fears the Lord, who obeys the voice of His Servant, yet who walks in darkness and deep trouble and has no shining splendor [in his heart]? Let him rely on, trust in, and be confident in the name of the Lord, and let him lean upon and be supported by his God.

The Lord said, *Nan, don't listen to the deceiver. He wants you to throw your hands up in defeat. I am the Sovereign Lord. I am absolute. Effectual. Guiding. Supreme. Nothing is too difficult for Me.*

I found myself holding that proverbial box again— the box mentioned in chapter six—the box we put God in from time to time. Do you remember? It was gilded in the finest gold, lined with the purest silver, and embellished with rubies, emeralds, sapphires, and diamonds. Nothing was too beautiful for the Lord. But once again, the Lord wanted to show me His magnificence. He wanted me to take Him out of the box. I realized that I was the one

Isaiah was referring to: I love the Lord, I do my best to walk in obedience to Him, and yet I find myself walking in darkness at times, living with a very dim heart. God, through Isaiah, exhorted me to rely upon His Name—that which speaks to the very essence of who He is. He is my Deliverer. My Redeemer. Savior. Mighty God. Counselor. Prince of Peace.

And if He is for me, then who can be against me?

In *Lord, I Want to Know You,* Kay Arthur wrote, "The children of Israel reacted over and over again to the circumstances of life rather than responding to the knowledge of God."[34] All of us are guilty of that sometimes. Perhaps it's human nature. Perhaps it boils down to the requisite of walking by faith and not by sight—to being in this world, but not of this world. Maybe. Probably. But this truth is more than a catchy phrase. This truth is phenomenal. This is the kind of truth that will set us free.

I've come to appreciate the sovereignty of God so much. It's hard to explain. When I understand—when you understand—that God is sovereign, then I understand that He's my constant in an ever-changing world. When I understand and take hold of the fact that He's the authority in my world and that nothing comes my way without His knowledge, I find peace. Yes, circumstances may take my breath away momentarily, but then I come back to my center and catch my balance. *El Elyon*—the sovereign Lord—is never taken by surprise by *anything* that happens to His child. He's aware of the difficulty or injustice long before it appears on our path. *El Elyon* has eternal purposes in all things, and He always has a plan. He rules supremely over all things.

Consider the story of Joseph, Jacob's eleventh son. His brothers were jealous of him and sold him into slavery to a passing caravan of Ishmaelites traveling to Egypt. Joseph was purchased by Potiphar, the captain of Pharaoh's guard. The Lord was with Joseph and gave him favor in his master's home. But then more injustice came. Potiphar's wife was attracted to Joseph and tried to seduce him. Joseph refused because of his loyalty to his master, but the wife sought revenge and implicated Joseph's guilt with lies. Joseph was thrown into prison for at least two years.

Did Joseph become bitter? No. Why not? Why didn't he become angry and disillusioned with God? Because Joseph didn't let his circumstances separate him from his knowledge of God. He had confidence in the Name of the Lord:

> The LORD was with Joseph and showed him mercy, and He gave him favor in the sight of the keeper of the prison ... The keeper of the prison did not look into anything that was under Joseph's authority, because the LORD was with him; and whatever he did, the LORD made it prosper. (Genesis 39:21, 23)

Even in prison.

Isn't it odd that Joseph suffered because he had been faithful to God? Actually, it's not—at least in biblical terms—but in our terms it's a different story, isn't it? Even though we've discussed at length the fellowship of the Lord's suffering, we still have this idea that bad things shouldn't happen to good people. Right? I know. I wrestle with it too. But the more I get to know *El Elyon*, the more I'm able to find eternal purposes in all things. I'm able to walk—I mean really walk—in the knowledge that all things work together for my good because I love God, and I'm called according to His purposes (Romans 8:28). That's why Joseph didn't grow bitter. He had been the victim of the wicked hearts of men, yet he did nothing to dishonor God. Joseph remained faithful.

Joseph was entrenched in the knowledge of God's sovereignty, and he relied on that knowledge. How do I know that? Look what happens next in this beloved Bible story. There is a great famine in the land. Because of God's hand on Joseph and his gift of dream interpretation, Pharaoh released him from prison and made him second in command over all of Egypt. Joseph was placed in charge of who received food and who didn't.

As the story progressed, Joseph's brothers came to Egypt looking for food. They stood before Joseph, who had full authority to determine if they received food, but they didn't recognize him. Joseph knew his brothers, though. With gut-wrenching sobs, he identified himself, and then he said:

> "But now, do not therefore be grieved or angry with yourselves because you sold me here; for God sent me before you to preserve life ... And God sent me before you to preserve a posterity for you in the earth, and to save your lives by a great deliverance ... But as for you,

you meant evil against me; but God meant it for good, in order to bring it about as it is this day, to save many people alive." (Genesis 45:5, 7, 8; 50:20)

What appears to us as a horrible circumstance in Joseph's life was overseen by a Sovereign Lord. His Presence never left Joseph during his imprisonment nor afterward. Joseph maintained his close relationship with *El Elyon* and, therefore, the Most High God could work through Joseph's circumstances to elevate him and weave him into an eternal plan.

I've been living this principle out loud in recent days—trusting in the sovereignty of my God, huddling under the protective armor of His authority in my life. Isn't it wonderful to know that all things work together for those who love Him and are called according to His purposes (Romans 8:28)? Yes and amen! All things, including broken hearts and broken lives. All things.

I look back over the past few years and see clearly how the Lord orchestrated pieces of my life so that when and if the time came, I'd be in a place of provision. By this, I mean that I believe the Lord knew temptation for marital infidelity was coming down the pike for David. The Lord promises that with every temptation He will provide a way of escape—if we so choose. Unfortunately, David got snared, leaving me in a million pieces. But my God was fully aware and had a plan.

I found myself in a financial crisis. Because of previous unemployment, we had no savings left. Although our finances had begun to turn around several months prior to the affair, we were still climbing out of a hole filled with quicksand. Our finances had a long way to go before they would provide solid footing. I haven't worked a secular job in several years so that I could serve alongside David and focus on my writing/speaking ministry. Consequently, in the natural sense, I found myself in a place of desolation. Confusion. Captive to my circumstances. I believe in a Sovereign God who puts all the pieces of our lives together with purpose and provision so ... what happened? How did His plan bring me to this horrid place? I stormed heaven with my accusations: I was angry. Hurt. Totally confused. *Lord, where are You? Why did You allow this to happen?*

I wish I had some profound declaration of faith for you at this juncture, but it took a while. I had no idea how dark the night of my soul was about to become. For weeks following the revelation of David's adultery, I grieved. I avoided public places in fear of what people were saying about us. Satan battered me with fiery darts of defeat and accusations of abandonment by the Lord I loved so much. My faith was shaken to its core, and my life on this earth was tossed about like crumpled paper in the wind. I had no income. None. Even though David was no longer living at home, he tried to help me, but he didn't have much to work with either. He had resigned from the pastorate and had begun working at a homeless shelter. I rolled coins and came up with thirty-eight dollars. That was it. I searched our home for items to sell—jewelry, family heirlooms, college rings. I applied for emergency food stamps. Each breath was filled with disbelief at what my life had become.

One day, all the ugly poured out in a hot mess of tears and anguish. I fell to my knees and proclaimed the goodness and faithfulness of the Lord. I affirmed that He had never left me nor forsaken me—that He was with me even in this dismal place:

God! I choose You. I trust You, Lord. You promise to work all things together for my good. I am trusting You to do that very thing in this painful place. I belong to You. You are my God. I don't know what tomorrow holds. I don't know how I will pay my bills, but I know that You know, and that's all that matters. I choose to take Your hand, to press into Your glorious Presence and live each moment as it comes, knowing that You are with me. Praise You, Lord. Thank You for Your faithfulness, mercy, and grace that is sufficient in all circumstances. Use this trial for Your glory.

An amazing thing happened: Jesus became my all in all.

My faith has taken on the wings of eagles as I wait on the Father to care for me and give me direction. How He sustains me is miraculous.

I find money in the mailbox, groceries on the front porch.

I suffered from bronchitis several weeks ago, and one day a box arrived in the mail containing a bottle of expensive cough syrup. Anonymously. That may not seem like much, but when you're down to nothing, an eight-dollar bottle of cough syrup costs a fortune. I was amazed.

A few months ago, my landlord offered me a part-time job at his restaurant to pay for my rent and electricity. He gave me hours that coordinated with my writing projects. Lee is eighty-four years old, so he's not up-to-date on things such as blogs and social media platforms that are necessary for writers and speakers. As I explained my dilemma and how much time it takes to build a platform publishers will accept, he listened to my heart and allowed God to use him to sustain me. I felt like so much had been stolen from me; I couldn't bear the thought of losing this part of my life too. I didn't expect to bring home a paycheck because of the money I owe Lee each month, but he insists that I need at least a little cash flow, so he always makes sure I bring home a portion of every check. What a blessing he has been in my life. I believe the Lord knew I would need this little farmhouse and my generous landlord long before the need was real. God used those years of unemployment to bring us home to our beloved mountains where we would find the home that Lee owned. The Lord knew He could trust Lee to help me.

Slowly, God's peace has permeated me. My worldly goods, as meager as they may have been to some, are gone. Do you remember when Paul remarked that he had lost everything to gain Christ? He wrote those words when he was in prison for spreading the gospel. I finally understand what he meant.

Paul said, *"Yet indeed I also count all things loss for the excellence of the knowledge of Christ Jesus my Lord, for whom I have suffered the loss of all things, and count them as rubbish, that I may gain Christ"* (Philippians 3:8). My sister, that happened to me. I literally lost everything material, but I gained the deep knowledge of the love of Christ. I'm learning of His faithfulness. His compassion. His joy. I'm learning to rest in His secret place. My faith has been proven to be more precious than gold, and for that I'm eternally grateful. The world can't take that away. Indeed, I've gained Christ and the knowledge of His love.

Like Paul, I'm beginning to move forward. Paul wrote, *Brethren, I do not count myself to have apprehended; but one thing I do, forgetting those things which are behind and reaching forward to those things which are ahead, I press toward the goal for the prize of the upward call of God in Christ Jesus* (Philippians 3:13-14). Never before have these familiar words meant so much to me. Never before have I put my hand to the plow and gripped it with such determination.

If God be for us, who can be against us?

You're going to laugh—I hope you laugh. As I was writing the previous paragraph, from deep within my memories I heard the following: "Like sand through the hourglass, so are the days of our lives." Are you old enough to remember that line? It's the opening line of the NBC soap opera, *Days of Our Lives*. Who knows why my brain triggered this response to understanding God's sovereignty, but hey, why not? Let's go with it.

I was actually thinking of a puzzle when that memory popped up: like pieces to a puzzle, so is the hand of God arranging our lives. I love the Lord's sense of humor, and I love how He gives us visuals to understand His lessons of grace. Our days tick away one by one, but unlike the soap opera, our days tick away with purpose. Each grain of sand and each puzzle piece is placed by His sovereign hand, right on time—a perfect fit, with a desired result.

I have a crazy quilt that my great-grandmother, Nancy Benson, quilted almost one hundred years ago. Odd pieces of fabric butt against one another. Various colors of embroidery floss weave their magic, securing the scraps and creating a glorious masterpiece.

Faith is like that. Faith in a sovereign God is absolutely like that. When we give Him the odd pieces—the scraps—of our lives and trust Him to secure the pieces together and create a masterpiece, we're walking in the knowledge of who He is and not in the knowledge of our circumstances. *Knowing* that God is creating a masterpiece from our brokenness enables us to accept His sovereignty and His authority, to believe His promise to work everything together for our good.

I've finally begun to take this Scripture to heart: *We are assured and know that [God being a partner in their labor] all things work together and are [fitting into a plan] for good to and for those who love God and are called according to [His] design and purpose* (Romans 8:28 AMP).

All things.

Not some.

All.

Oh, that we would open our eyes to see. Injustices juxtaposed against His truth, despair butted against His hope, fear stitched to His peace—all joined by the scarlet thread of Jesus' blood, all woven according to His eternal purposes—His plan unfolding.

Oh my goodness. Dear sister, may your heart be stirred to embrace this knowledge of His grace. What an amazing God we serve. His love is beyond comprehension.

And, if God be for us, who can be against us? *Elohim*, the Creator of the Universe, calls us His child. We're the apple of His eye. The God who holds the seas in the hollow of His hands, the God who rides on the wings of the wind, the One who speaks and the demons themselves tremble—if He is for us, who would dare to be against us?

The Lord is calling me to a deeper place.

Perhaps He's calling you, as well.

He's calling me to that perfect place of refuge beneath the shadow of His wing. He's calling me to rest in the knowledge that He's with me—always—to get that in my *knower* so that when the enemy assails me I won't be afraid. He's opening my eyes to see and understand that, just as He is in me, I am in Him, completely surrounded by His Presence. If this wasn't true, how else could we respond to His request, "Come to Me"? He is our portion. He is our place of shelter and comfort. We belong to Him.

The Lord spoke through the prophet Isaiah:

"Fear not, for I have redeemed you; I have called you by name; you are mine. When you pass through the waters, I will be with you; and when you pass through the rivers, they will not sweep over you. When you walk through the fire you will not be burned; the flames will not set you ablaze. For I am the LORD your God, the Holy One of Israel your Savior." (Isaiah 43:1-3 NIV)

In further exhortation, the Lord spoke through the psalmist, *"Be still, and know that I am God"* (Psalm 46:10). Can you hear the Lord saying, "Calm down, my child. I am God. Nothing is coming to you without coming past me first." How many times have we said these words to our own children or to a loved one? "Calm down. It's going to be okay."

I'm learning to calm down, to sit still. I'm learning to look around and see the evidence of God's power in my midst. When I take a minute to remember His faithfulness, the times He has provided for me, the times He has filled me with hope when I was engulfed in despair—when I take time to do this, my spirit settles down. My mind stops thrashing about in the crisis. Each of us must learn to let be—to be still.

In the stillness, we understand that He is God and that if He hung the stars in the sky, surely He can make everything okay for us.

Recently, after an especially long, grueling day, I felt a familiar tug on my heart. It was the Holy Spirit bidding me to come, wooing me with His love. I sat in His Presence. As I prayed, I listened. I opened my heart and tuned my ear to His voice:

My child, Your hope is in Me, the Creator, the God above all gods. No other is like Me. I ride upon the heavens to help you. My eyes search the earth for those I might strengthen. Yes, your hope is in Me. I will never fail you; I will never forsake you—you are Mine. My glories I will reveal. My truth I will impart. You are my precious child, My treasure. I hold you near to My heart, near to My love. Draw near to Me, and I will draw near to you with a response of love and care and surety. I order your steps. I guide you by the Light of My Word. Do not stray to the left nor to the right. No, keep your eyes on Me and I shall direct your paths. You are Mine. I desire your happiness, your joy. Give me your burdens—they are much too heavy for you to bear. You feel so small and insignificant, but never forget: I AM with you and in Me all the earth has its being. I love you, My precious one. You are Mine and I am yours.

He is our God—hallelujah! He is sovereign over all things. When we walk closely with the Lord, we're completely surrounded by His Presence—we're living within His love. We're safe. We're complete. No weapon formed against us can prosper because no weapon can penetrate His shield.

So, what do you think? With God on our side like this, how can we lose? If God didn't hesitate to put everything on the line for us, embracing our condition and exposing Himself to the worst by sending His own Son, is there anything else He wouldn't gladly and freely do for us? And who would dare tangle with God by messing with one of God's chosen? Who would dare even to point a finger? The One who died for us—who was raised to life for us!—is in the presence of God at this very moment sticking up for us. Do you think anyone is going to be

able to drive a wedge between us and Christ's love for us?
There is no way! Not trouble, not hard times, not hatred,
not hunger, not homelessness, not bullying threats, not
backstabbing ... None of this fazes us because Jesus loves
us. I'm absolutely convinced that nothing—nothing
living or dead, angelic or demonic, today or tomorrow,
high or low, thinkable or unthinkable—absolutely
nothing can get between us and God's love because of the
way that Jesus our Master has embraced us. (Romans
8:31-35, 37-39 MSG)

My precious sister, you are loved by an amazing God.
You honor Him with your life of service—with your
willingness to undergird your husband during the best of
times and during the worst of times. Step with confidence
into your tomorrows knowing this: the Lord your God is
for you and He is with you. Always.

May I share one final prayer with you?

Father God, You have taken us on a phenomenal journey.
You have walked with us, spoken with us, and carried us
into a new understanding of Your Presence in our lives.
Thank You so much. Thank You for having a heart that
is turned toward Your children, especially those who fight
on the front lines for the advancement of the gospel. We
take comfort in the knowledge that You are our Deliverer,
our Refuge, our Counselor, and our God.

I bring my sister before Your throne of grace. As she bows
before You, I ask that You touch her by the power of

Your Holy Spirit. Grant her a fresh anointing to walk in her Calling—boldness to face the enemy square on and remind him to Whom she belongs. Rise up within her, Lord. Fill her with laughter and purpose, strength and an abundance of grace. We love You, Lord. Be glorified in our lives as we, your daughters, carry Your love to a hurting world. Praise You, Father. In Jesus' name I pray, amen.

STRENGTH FOR THE JOURNEY

A Final Note from Nan

I'M SO HONORED that you've joined hands with me on this journey toward healing. I've created a downloadable pdf containing a compilation of "Promises for the Perils of a Pastor's Wife" for your convenience. In the file, I've included additional Scriptures for each peril. If you're like me, my Bible is chock-full of inspirational notes. I hope you'll add these promises to your stash. To access this link, go to my website at NanJones.com and click on Freebies. Other resources are also available there.

As my reader and my sister in the Lord, you're very important to me. I'd love to hear from you.

Contact me at:

- email: nan@jubilantlight.com
- website: NanJones.com
- devotional blog, Morning Glory at http://morningglorylights.blogspot.com/, which addresses finding God's presence in all things that pertain to us.

And, of course, we can't leave out social media.

For Twitter, find me at @NanJonesAuthor; Pinterest at Nan Jones http://www.pinterest.com/nantjones/, LinkedIn at Nan Jones Christian Writer and Speaker, and on Facebook, Nan Trammell Jones. It would thrill my heart to connect with you. Even on social media, I encourage those like me who sometimes struggle with faith because of life's difficulties. My social platform is filled with reminders that God is with us. Always.

One last thing. Please spread the news about *The Perils of a Pastor's Wife*. Help me get it into the hands of our sisters who are struggling with ministry. Word of mouth is always great. Recommending the book to other pastors' wives or encouraging friends and family to consider purchasing *The Perils of a Pastor's Wife* for the pastors' wives in their lives would be wonderful. Also, consider mentioning *The Perils of a Pastor's Wife* on Facebook or Twitter—wherever you gather with friends. Please prayerfully consider writing a review on Amazon or Goodreads. You, my reader, have the power to make or break a book. A review doesn't have to be long—just a sentence or two about your response to the book's message and, hopefully, your recommendation.

Thank you so much for reading *The Perils of a Pastor's Wife*. I cherish your prayers as I work to spread its message.

You are a blessing to me,

Nan Jones

Endnotes

Chapter 1: After the Fire, a Gentle Whisper

[1] Jack W. Hayford, general editor, Sam Middlebrook, Old Testament editor, and Jerry Horner, New Testament editor. *Spirit Filled Life Bible.* (Nashville: Thomas Nelson Publishers, 1991), 517.

Chapter 4: The Fellowship of His Sufferings

[2] *Spirit Filled Life Bible*, 1628.

[3] "Know the Truth," Hands for Jesus, May 30, 2008, www.handsforjesus.org/KnowT2.htm.

[4] "Philippians 3," Barnes' Notes, accessed July, 2013, biblehub.com/commentaries/barnes/philippians/3.htm.

Chapter 5: Greater Is He That Is in Me

[5] *Spirit Filled Life Bible*, 1946.

[6] *Spirit Filled Life Bible*, 1540.

[7] *Spirit Filled Life Bible*, 1863.

[8] "Lesson 7: The Sword of the Spirit, The Word of God," Bible Study Guides: Practical Answers, Real Hope, accessed July, 2013, www.freebiblestudyguides.org/bible-teachings/armor-of-god-sword-of-spirit-word.htm.

[9] *Spirit Filled Life Bible*, 1408.

[10] *Spirit Filled Life Bible*, 1797.

[11] *Spirit Filled Life Bible*, 1108.

Chapter 6: Joy in the Wilderness

[12] Hannah Hurnard, *Hinds' Feet on High Places*, (Illinois: Living Books/ Tyndale House Publishers, Inc., 2006), 89-91.

[13] "Psalm 16," Pulpit Commentary, accessed July 2013, www.pulpit. biblecommenter.com/psalms/16.htm.

[14] Frances J. Roberts, *Come Away My Beloved* (Uhrichsville: Barbour Publishing, 2002), 103.

Chapter 7: Come to Me

[15] Beth Moore, *A Woman's Heart: God's Dwelling Place* (Nashville: LifeWay Press, 2007), 36.

[16] "Commentary on Isaiah 51:1-6, Ingrid Lilly, August 21, 2011, http://www.workingpreacher.org/preaching.aspx?commentary_ id=1050

[17] *Spirit Filled Life Bible*, 1011.

[18] Robert Young, LL.D., *Young's Analytical Concordance to the Bible* (McLean: MacDonald Publishing Co., 1984), 188.

Chapter 8: The Secret Place beneath His Wings

[19] George Bennard, *Baptist Hymnal*. (Nashville: Convention, Print, 1991), 141.

[20] *Spirit Filled Life Bible*, 391-392.

[21] *Spirit Filled Life Bible*, 131.

[22] *Spirit Filled Life Bible*, 902.

[23] *Spirit Filled Life Bible*, 1344.

Chapter 9: Stand by Your Man

[24] Barbara Ann Kipfer and Princeton Language Institute, *Roget's 21st Century Thesaurus in Dictionary Form: The Essential Reference for Home, School, or Office* (New York: Dell Publishers, 1999. Print), 616.

[25] Stormie Omartian, *The Power of a Praying Wife* (Eugene: Harvest House Publishers, 1997), 95.

[26] Omartian, *The Power of a Praying Wife*, 199-200.

Chapter 10: I Didn't See It Coming

[27] Omartian, *The Power of a Praying Wife*, 199-200.

[28] "12 Inspirational Rick Warren Quotes on Forgiveness," posted by befruitful, 7/16/14, http://ipost.christianpost.com/news/12-inspirational-rick-warren-quotes-on-forgiveness-15119/

[29] Anne Lamott, *Traveling Mercies: Some Thoughts on Faith* (New York: Anchor Books, 1999. Print), 134.

[30] Into Thy Word/Statistics on Pastors. Dr. Richard J. Krejcir (borrowed from the *Francis A. Schaeffer Institute of Church Leadership Development*. www.intothyword.org/apps/articles/?articledid=36562.)

[31] L.B. Cowman. Edited by Jim Reimann, *Streams in the Desert*, (Grand Rapids: Zondervan, 1997), 344-345.

[32] Marcell Warner Bridges© 27 September 2014. Used by permission.

Chapter 11: If God Be for Me

[33] Barbara Ann Kipfer and Princeton Language Institute, *Roget's 21st Century Thesaurus*, 674.

[34] Kay Arthur, *Lord, I Want to Know You*, (Colorado Springs, Colorado: Waterbrook Press, 2002), 93.